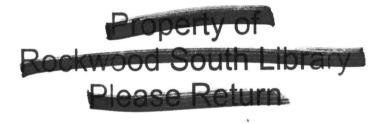

Breakfast
with
the Pope

Breakfast
with
the Pope

SUSAN VIGILANTE

RICHARD VIGILANTE BOOKS

PUBLISHED BY RICHARD VIGILANTE BOOKS
Copyright © 2010 by Susan Vigilante
All Rights Reserved
www.richardvigilantebooks.com
RVB with the portrayal of a Labrador retriever in profile is a trademark
of Richard Vigilante Books
Book design by Charles Bork
Library of Congress Control Number: 2010912861

Applicable BISAC Codes:
REL012120   RELIGION / Christian Life / Spiritual Growth
OCC019000   BODY, MIND & SPIRIT / Inspiration & Personal Growth
BIO018000   BIOGRAPHY & AUTOBIOGRAPHY / Religious

ISBN 978-0-9800763-8-7
PRINTED IN THE UNITED STATES OF AMERICA
10 9 8 7 6 5 4 3 2 1
First Edition

For Mary Beth, Harry, Dean, and Emma

CONTENTS

PART IV
Be Not Afraid

This is the story as I remember it. Others in the story have their own memories and their own stories. For that reason I have changed the names of several of the most important characters, not so much to conceal their identities, but to honor the truth that their memories, their stories are different from mine. So friends, when you come to "your" character and say, "that is not how it was, that is not me at all" we can acknowledge that truth together. Be at peace. My memory of you is not you and goes by another name.

PART I
Sharon

I

"Teléfono Vaticani," says the light, lovely recorded female voice. "Vi preghiamo di attendere." A moment later a second voice, this one with a prim British accent, offers a translation. "Vatican telephones. Please hold on."

I hold on until finally a brusque, live Italian operator picks up. "Pronto?"

I blurt out the first of the two lines I've been rehearsing since I started dialing ten minutes ago. "Palazzo papale a Castel Gandolfo, per favore." Which means, more or less, "Please connect me with the papal palace at Castel Gandolfo."

I've made this call before. As usual the operator breaks off before I get to the "per favore," and I get the obnoxious sound of a European telephone trying to connect, something between a buzz and a honk. HOZONK. HOZONK. HOZOOOOOONK...

Finally another voice answers, this one male and even more brusque than the last one. "Pronto!" (Supposedly this is how Italians say "hello," but at this number it usually comes across as something more like "whaddaya want?")

I blurt out my second line. "Prego, parlare con la dottoressa Pawlowska, per fa—"

HOZONK. HOZONK. HOZOOOOOONK . . .

Now comes the wild card of the whole endeavor. This is the point where anything could happen. I might wait only a few seconds before the man who answers the phone breaks in and snaps in Italian: "They're not here, call later," and hangs up. Or I might just hold on, listening to the buzz-honk for another fifteen minutes before I finally admit defeat. Or, if I'm really lucky, someone might actually answer the phone.

That could be any one of half a dozen people.

It could be *La Dottoressa* herself, who may not remember me, is a bit scary, not particularly patient, and not at all reluctant to act on her first instincts. It could be her philosophy professor husband, who certainly will not remember me but won't care. We might have a perfectly pleasant chat. But since he will forget all about me as soon as he puts the phone down, there will be no point leaving a message and I'll have to repeat the whole exercise later.

Or—and this is hitting the jackpot, this almost never happens—it could be one of the people I am trying to reach: my friend Kasia Zajac, with her husband Stanislaw, and their two sons, Walter and Charlie.

It wasn't always so hard to reach them by phone. When they lived in the Bronx and we lived in Queens, we shared an area code. In this tiny Italian resort town every attempt at telecommunication is an adventure.

Kasia always said that the key to a successful call to the palazzo was patience. "Let it ring," she said. "This is an old baroque palace. Many corridors, few telephones. I tell you nothing is more frustrating than thinking you hear a phone ringing, then running miles down those corridors, only to have the person hang up when you get there. Let it ring."

I let it ring and ring but no one answers. I check my watch. It's past three; they're taking a longer lunch than usual. Finally the operator breaks into my reverie. "They're not home. Call later." He cuts me off. And by "later" he means much later: after lunch comes siesta, so I won't be able to call again for hours.

So much for the miracle of fiber optics. Actually the miracle of tin can and string would have done just as well, since the palace is not two hundred yards from where I'm standing right now, in the parlor of the tiny Hotel Bucci.

"Any luck?" my husband asks.

"Nope." On a scrap torn from a notebook I write, "Kasia! We are at the Hotel B. We'll be on the piazza after siesta. Hope Stan told you we were coming! Love, Susan and Rich." I fold the note and write on the outside, "Pawlowska/Zajac. From the Vigilantes."

With note in hand Richard and I pick our way up the narrow cobblestone street. The midday meal is drawing to a close; we can tell from the clearing-the-table clatter spilling out from every window. In fifteen minutes most of the town will be closed until the late afternoon. I only hope there is still someone on duty at the palace gate.

But when we reach the square the gate is already closed. "Great," my husband mutters, crabby from the combined effects of the heat, jet lag, and the jitters that stay with us long after we have pulled off the Auto-strada. "Now how will we get hold of them?"

"I'm going to knock," I reply. "Someone's got to be there." I say this knowing it is not true. This is Italy. Nothing "has to be" here.

We cross the piazza, passing the church and the fountain and the outdoor cafés on the way to our destination, the *palazzo papale*, the "papal palace," the summer residence of the popes since 1604. The tiny piazza is dominated on the north by the south wall of the palace, which itself is quite simple and seems large only because everything else in Castel Gandolfo is so small. The façade is a golden yellow stucco; over the great wooden gates in the center are a pair of large, usually shuttered windows from which the Holy Father could greet a crowd in the piazza, although usually he does not. Instead at appointed times—for the Angelus on Sunday, or the Friday Night Rosary—the crowds are admitted through the front gates and gather in the courtyard that forms the center of the palace grounds. The Holy Father presides from an interior balcony just on the opposite side of the same room from which those shuttered windows look out to the piazza.

Simple as the palace is walking up to the front door is an imposing task. The broad façade is like a huge backdrop on an unadorned stage. And to get to the gate you must ascend a steep incline from the piazza. Unless there is a huge crowd milling about, which there isn't, except when a crowd is lined up to get in for the rosary or a public mass or the Angelus, you cannot walk up to the gate inconspicuously. You feel exposed, as if everyone on the square, in the cafés, in the shops, the post office is watching you. This feeling is entirely accurate. Not only is this small town as gossipy as any, in the summer it is a court. And no gossip is as precious as an eyewitness account of any doings at court, including the odd sight of two Americans walking up to the very solidly shut front gate and . . . knocking. It occurs to me, too late, that I am going to look pretty foolish if no one answers.

Trying very hard to look as if I do this every day, which is very hard since really no one does this on almost any day, I knock on the ancient oak doors. Unlike the phones, the answer to a human knock is quick. A Swiss Guard in full Renaissance plummage opens the narrow door within the gate and steps out. Like most of the Swiss Guard he could be a male model or a professional athlete, a centerfielder maybe, long-limbed with plenty of muscle but no extra bulk to cut down his range, and a face made for endorsements.

"Sera." A hint of casualness in the manner, but no smile, as if to say, "although I'm not at the moment going to impale you on one of the several medieval yet remarkably effective weapons I have just behind me, Signora, please understand that I am in charge here."

"Buona sera," I reply, trying to match the seriousness of his tone, always a good idea when dealing with a man who owns a halberd. The formalities over, I repeat the most important Italian phrase I know, "Lei parla inglese?"

"Si, yes." I hand him the note and explain my mission. There is some confusion at first: He is not sure who the Zajacs are. He calls something over his shoulder and another Swiss Guard emerges from the guardhouse. They confer briefly before the second one says, "Oh, that's the daughter."

"Yes," we say. "The one with the two boys. You know Walter? And Charlie? You must know Charlie."

The guards exchange glances; one says something in Italian. They both laugh. They know Charlie, all right. A typical reaction. And he is still only eight.

They promise me they will see that Kasia gets my note. We thank them and head back to the Bucci to laze off a little jet lag.

By the end of siesta we still have not heard anything from our friends. We rouse ourselves anyway and set about a few errands. We change some money at the post office and buy stamps for postcards. We buy Richard a straw hat to protect him from the sun, a cheap one the boys can toss into the fountain and otherwise abuse when the urge takes them. Then the most important task of all: we select a table on the piazza and sit, not to wait, but just to be. At first we can't quite manage it.

"Are you sure they know we're coming?" Richard asks as we settle at a table.

"I told Stanislaw," I answer evasively. "I wrote him a letter."

"You sent it to Bulgaria?" Stan teaches at a university there.

"Yes. And I called Kasia's father in Kraków. I told him too."

"I see."

I do not reply. Richard is right, of course. Between Kasia's head-in-the-clouds father and the Bulgarian postal system I have no idea if the Zajacs ever heard we were coming. I just hope the Swiss Guard won't let me down.

After a while a waiter stops at our table. We order mineral water, the cheapest thing on the menu, which will allow us to sit there indefinitely, listening to the water playing in the fountain and watching the little world of Castel Gandolfo go by. It does for several hours, but try as we can to relax, to sink into Italy, we can't help looking up again and again as people come and go, to search for our friends, who were never among them.

Finally Richard put his book aside. "You want to go get some dinner?"

There are two parts to the Hotel Bucci. The inn, which takes up most of the building and the down-the-alley-and-around-the-back part, where the restaurant is. The restaurant and the hotel proper are separately owned and operated by different branches of the same family.

We liked the hotel part but we loved the restaurant. Small, with a long balcony lined with tables overlooking the lake, it had one tiny kitchen and one magnificent cook. On a crowded night dinner might appear at a leisurely pace, but it was always worth the wait. There were only a handful of dishes on the menu, all apparently extremely simple, but somehow exploding with flavor. We got a table and ordered the trout, which is sautéed in olive oil with sage and rosemary and I assume white wine, and is the best trout either of us has ever eaten, and which we have never been able to recreate at home, though we have tried repeatedly. While we waited we sipped some local wine and gazed down at the lake.

Crew teams were practicing on the water. The Lago Albano was one of the sites for the Rome Olympics in 1962. It is still a popular place among athletes, and in the summer it hosts any number of rowing competitions. The daughter of the woman who was at that moment preparing our trout competed sometimes.

I

We talked about plans for the week: a drive to Frascati, a couple of days in Rome, swimming at the lake. And as much time with Kasia and the boys as we could get.

As guests of the Holy Father, Kasia and her family had full schedules. They had to appear for all meals, properly dressed. Kasia and her mother were often called upon to act as interpreters for visiting dignitaries. And of course there was the summer reading list.

One of the things John Paul II liked to do on his vacations was catch up on his reading. There was so much he wanted to read, though, that even he—a man with a couple of doctorates and command of eight or nine languages—couldn't manage it all on his own. So he would often read two books at once, one in the conventional way while another was read to him at the same time by one of our friends. We always prayed he would give Kasia a good one. One year she got a history of witchcraft trials in medieval Germany that was so boring the Holy Father had to apologize for sticking her with it. Even so it put her in a foul mood for days.

After we polished off our trout we picked at a bowl of fruit. The local peach festival had wrapped just a week or two before, and the peaches, served on ice, were enormous and sweet and pouring with juice. Pair them with a couple of biscotti and you were in paradise.

"So what do you think?" said Richard. "Should we try the palace again?"

"I doubt anyone will answer. They're probably still at dinner, anyway."

"Well, we can give it another try in the morning." He covered a yawn. "Feel like doing some reading?"

"Yes. But let's go up to the square."

Castel Gandolfo's Piazza della Libertà is small, beautiful, and one of our favorite places to be. The gold stucco façade of the palace forms the northern edge of the square; the western side is all cafés and small shops. On the other side are the post office, one or two more shops, and the Church of St. Thomas of Villanova. Designed by Bernini, the church's simple façade, a modest but perfectly proportioned Greek cross and dome, conceals one of the most dramatic interiors he ever created. I wonder how many tourists never step inside, deceived that they are passing one more simple Italian country church.

Everywhere there are terracotta pots overflowing with flowers.

In the center of the piazza there is a marble fountain. On the yellow and black signs one sees all over Italy at the main entryways into a town, the fountain is listed as one of Castel Gandolfo's three official tourist sites: *Palazzo Papale*, obviously the number-one attraction, *Etruscan Necropolis*, and *Fontana Bernini*.

Bernini created four famous fountains. Every tourist to Rome has seen at least two of them, the Fountain of the Four Rivers and the Fontana del Moro, not originally Bernini's but made famous by his sculpture of "the Moor" that so dominates Giacomo della Porta's original scheme. Both can be seen from the tour bus stop at the Piazza Navona. The fountain in the piazza at Castel Gandolfo bears no resemblance to either, and its authorship is disputed, which may be why the signs are so insistent.

Like the façade of the church, the fountain is simple but full of grace. A pedestal of four female figures facing the points of the compass rises perhaps five feet above a three-foot-high rounded octagonal pool, which I would guess is about nine feet in diameter. Resting atop the pedestal of the four women is a simple shallow basin, perfectly proportioned to the pool below, out of which four streams of water, no thicker or more forceful than might come from your garden hose, arch with a gentle noise into the pool. At night the fountain is illuminated with electric lights.

The Barberini fountain in Rome, another of the famous ones and undeniably Bernini, is also simple and in my memory no larger. The Castel Gandolfo fountain is prettier, in part because it doesn't have those goofy Barberini bees. But I think it is also because the four streams of water dropping so simply and functionally into the serene abundance of the pool below speak more powerfully than any of the master's more famous works of the Italian reverence for and delight in water, recorded repeatedly in statute as well as statuary from the early Roman Republic on.

It is one of the most beautiful and characteristic things about Italy, this love of fountains. In this hot, dry, drought-prone climate, water is a very serious business. Of all Roman engineering works the aqueducts are the most impressive and difficult to credit as the work of an ancient people with only muscle power driving their machines and far more impressive than the celebrated roads. Water-rights disputes were a motif of Roman law and politics. There was even a system of precedents for acquiring legal title to leaks from Rome's municipal water pipes so that if the authorities sealed up a leak to which a Roman citizen had developed a rightful claim he could poke it open again.

So there the Romans are, desperate for water, driving themselves to engineering feats to shame the gods, in a brutal physical labor, some of which at least was undertaken by free men before Rome had a large slave population, and what do they make? Free public baths and fountains, fountains everywhere as if they had all the water in the four rivers flowing through their streets. To this day Italians celebrate scarcity with shows of abundance. What we call water fountains — where you press the button to make the stream flow for drinking — are hardly ever seen. But the city is full of small decorative fountains, always flowing, helpfully marked *"potabile"* for thirsty travelers.

Italians are not wasteful. They are in most ways as thrifty as any Yankee. They drive tiny cars, eat what seem to us tiny meals, and live in tiny houses, in which they seem never to turn on the electricity. But both Italian thrift and Italian prodigality are of a type so unlike ours that they take some time to grasp. Where the necessities of life are concerned they are by comparison to Americans absolutely Spartan; but for luxury, for display, for delight, for beauty, then nothing should be spared. The aesthetic has as much moral force in most of Italy as commerce has for us, and ugliness or meanness in display seems as scandalous to them as extravagance in business seems to us.

The first time this came home to us in full force was one time when we were in Assisi. We had been walking about the city all day, doing more shopping than usual, in part because we tend to do a lot of window shopping in Umbria because of the pottery, but mostly for the pleasure of extending our walk through one of the prettiest medieval towns in Italy. It's simply not true, by the way, that Assisi is spoiled by tourists. For one thing, they are not tourists but pilgrims and have been going there in comparable numbers for almost a thousand years, on and off. They don't spoil Assisi; they are as essential to it as the Basilica and have been since anyone cared that there was an Assisi.

We stopped in maybe a dozen shops that day and in every shop, even in the most dim and narrow streets, the lights were off. In most shops even the fans were not turning. Richard is a publisher and he admires good marketing. So he pointed this out in something of a huff, muttering that it would be better business to let people know your shop was open, or maybe even actually light the display cases and show your wares to best advantage.

We walked until twilight, ascending all the way to the great fortress, the Rocca, which tops the hill on which the old city sits, perhaps a thousand feet above the plain below. As the sun set we began down again. The shops were mostly closed now, and by the time we had descended to the plain it was full dark. We were tired and hungry, focused on finding the car, and I think bickering about whether to look for dinner locally or go back to San Gemini where we were staying. Perhaps to end the argument, before getting into the car we turned around for one last look at the old city.

It was shining. The entire hill burned with light. Every light in the city, and they clearly had far more lights than we ever suspected, must have been lit. Especially in contrast to the surrounding near total darkness (Umbria is still quite rural) it was a display rivaling any fireworks we had ever seen in DC on the Fourth—and Washington does the best fireworks in the world. It was not a feast day; it was not even Sunday. It wasn't to light the streets or show off the shops or for any practical reason at all, because by then the old city was almost empty and all the shops were closed. It was for beauty and delight and on the whole an excellent use of electricity.

In this little fountain Bernini gave Castel Gandolfo its playground, its campfire, its excuse to stay up half the night talking. The fountain is the heart of the square, especially at night, when the gates of the palazzo are shut and the looming yellow façade fades into the shadows. The sounds of the water splashing from the pipes into the pool are the background music for dozens of conversations, memories, plans, secrets. It is the continuo beneath the late-night philosophy discussions between Richard and the various professors. It is the soundtrack to the private little movie Kasia and I have watched together more than once, *What The Swiss Guard Do After Hours*. (They sit around in faded jeans and polo shirts, looking gorgeous. It's a great movie.)

The palace may be more imposing and San Tommaso a far greater expression of Bernini's art, but even the pope comes to Castel Gandolfo to play. Bernini, they say, gave Rome its face. But he gave this little town its heart.

Something white flickered in the corner of my eye. I turned just in time to see a long, willowy form being swallowed up by the palace gates.

I dropped my book. The table wobbled sharply on the cobblestones.

Richard looked up from his reading. "Hey!"

"Sorry." I bent over to pick up my book. "You know what, I'm really pretty tired. I'd like to go back."

"OK." We paid our tab and left.

Richard fell asleep almost immediately; I lay awake. When I got tired of staring at the ceiling I got up and went out onto the balcony.

The night was hot and muggy. The sky was dense with humidity, and only a handful of stars was visible above the lake. Gazing into the darkness I contemplated what I had seen back at the piazza.

I'd know that long, willowy figure anywhere. That was Kasia going through those gates. What was more, I know she saw me too. And she had turned away.

II

The first time we came to Italy was in the summer of 1992.

We had been talking for years about going some day. Richard is Italian on his father's side; his grandparents came from a village near Naples. Richard's older brother, my brother-in-law Kevin, went to medical school in Rome for three years before coming home to New York and finishing his education at New York Hospital–Cornell Medical Center. His sister Mary had spent a semester abroad studying art history in Urbino. My sister and brother-in-law had gone to Rome on their honeymoon and come back raving about it. Even the Queens neighborhood we lived in was heavily Italian; you could still hear bits of dialect bawled across the alleyways, and the local deli and dairy stores stocked the kinds of Italian delicacies then still hard to find in most neighborhoods. I, like so many full-blooded Irish Americans, had been thrilled to marry into a culture whose cuisine incorporated actual flavors and textures other than dried out and limp.

Still, we had no firm plans to travel. We were young. And we seemed to ourselves even younger, both because we had no children and because we were both still struggling to get our professional lives started. We were both writers so we were frequently broke, but we were too long out of college for the backpack and hitchhike scene. Richard in any event is deeply devoted to indoor plumbing. Vacationing in Europe seemed farfetched.

Then Ross Perot re-entered the presidential race.

Although we had never really considered it seriously, there was this one little possibility that had occasionally been discussed. One of our closest friends, Lee, worked in the (first) Bush White House. In the course of one of the most trying times in the Bush administration, the Clarence Thomas nomination, she had become good friends with another Bushie, Mark, who in turn was a friend and protégé of the U.S. ambassador to the Vatican.

The ambassador, like most Romans with any choice in the matter, fled the city in August. Since the residence would be empty, he had told Mark a few years before that if he could get to Italy during late August he could stay there. Mark in turn had offered to include Lee in his good fortune, and Lee in turn had mentioned it to us.

In the summer of 1992, when Perot re-entered the race, it became clear that after November the offer would expire. Lee called us one day in late June. "If we're going to go to Italy we have to go now," she said bluntly. (Lee is a never-say-die type who rarely left the

White House before ten PM, so the Bushies must have been in real despair.) Three weeks later the three of us were on a nonstop flight to Fiumicino Airport.

Even with the almost free place to stay in Rome, our vacation was painfully expensive. But despite a rotten exchange rate and a heat wave the likes of which Romans had not seen in years, it was impossible not to fall in love with Italy. We did St. Peter's and saw the *Pieta*; we went to San Paolo fuori le Mura and counted the mosaics of the popes above the pillars of the nave. (It is said that when all the spaces are filled the papacy will end and the end times begin.)We took the bus out to the catacombs where we had a picnic lunch and agreed on a new rule: never dine downwind of a bunch of Frenchmen. We heard *Aida* at the Baths of Caracalla in a performance that included the chorus marching into the amphitheatre armed with torches and spears and executing a superb flanking maneuver around the audience, giving us no choice but surrender or flight. (We chose flight. I hate that opera. Lee is a Mozart girl.) We tossed pennies in the Trevi fountain. We took the train to Florence and a bus to Assisi; we spent a day in Siena and a shameful amount of time just sitting around cafés, which we all agreed was our favorite Italian thing to do, dreamily scheming how we could come back to live in Rome.

We spent only one day with the Zajacs that summer. We had known them for several years by then. Kasia had become one of my closest friends and the boys, wild about

Richard, had adopted us as honorary aunt and uncle. But it was our first time in the country, and we were intent on being tourists. (Anyone who comes to Italy and refuses ever to play the tourist is not a sophisticate but a philistine—and a fool.) The Zajacs were never coy about their relationship with Karol Wojtyla. Kasia's earliest childhood memory is of the young priest playfully lifting her up in the air and perching her on top of a chest of drawers or a mantelpiece. But they were naturally reserved about it, and we naturally hesitant to inquire. So, for instance, we had no idea that Castel Gandolfo itself is one of the most delightful places to be in Italy.

Still Kasia and Stan had insisted so often that we stop and see them that we had no fear they were being merely polite (or, as they would say, being American) and had promised we would. One day Lee broke down and admitted she really did have to do some work and toddled off to use the fax and phones at the American embassy. So Richard and I took the train from Roma Termini to Castel Gandolfo, roughly a forty-five minute ride past towering aqueducts, into the the hill country outside Rome, the "castelli" (for castles) region, home to the summer estates of the wealthy and powerful of the city for more than two thousand years.

On the train a young conductor glanced over our tickets. "You going to see the big guy?" he asked casually.

We laughed. "Yeah. Sure."

He nodded and punched the tickets. "Tell him I said 'hi,'" he said, moving on to the next passenger.

Castel Gandolfo is about eighteen miles southeast of Rome, but about thirteen hundred feet higher, perched on the western rim of a defunct volcano high above an impossibly blue and beautiful volcanic lake. The train station is on the volcanic slope about halfway between the town and the lake. The climb up to town is only a few hundred feet, but it is extremely steep, occasionally scary, and on that blistering day a sweaty, miserable, and intimidating walk. We stopped half a dozen times to catch our breath, each time turning to look down on the lake, each time resisting the urge to tear down the hill and throw ourselves into the water. We didn't; we were too horrified at the idea of climbing back up.

Parched and irritable we reached the top and followed the signs to the town center. As we staggered onto the piazza we saw Kasia waving to us from a café table. When we got a little closer she burst out laughing.

"Susan, Richard, you look like death! Sit down. Drink some mineral water. I will order some *granita*." (The Italian version of a snow cone except delicious.) Richard wasn't waiting. In the middle of the piazza was Bernini's small marble fountain. Richard made a beeline for it. He stuck his hands under one of the streams and splashed his face with cold water. Then he looked slowly around the square for the first time. And he smiled.

The papal estate at Castel Gandolfo has a long history, only part of it involving popes. Emperor Domitian had his summer villa there, and the vast formal gardens include a small but well-preserved amphitheatre as well as stretches of Roman roads. The papacy acquired the estate from the Savelli family in 1596. Pope Urban VIII hired the architect Carlo Maderno to design his summer palace, which was built in 1624. Today the estate covers about 135 acres, most of which are devoted to the gardens in which Kasia had gotten permission for us to spend the afternoon.

"Holy Father is not coming out today," she said as we strolled down an avenue lined with citrus trees. "He is not feeling very well."

"He has the flu," one of the boys piped up.

"He has a cold," Kasia corrected.

"A bad one," said the younger boy.

"He wouldn't feel so bad if they let him use the air conditioning," Walter, the older boy, muttered. "It's too hot in the palace. We can hardly breathe."

"But the doctors will only let him use the air conditioning if he keeps all the windows open!" Charlie gestured his amazed disgust. The care of the Holy Father's health was a subject of furious debate and politicking between various factions, often producing apparently absurd and contradictory decisions. Health care by committee. No, worse. By an Italian committee.

Kasia said something in Polish. The boys shot ahead of us, racing each other along the graveled path.

"Anyway, I am sorry you cannot meet him," she said. "He sends his greetings, though."

Never having expected to meet him we were duly awed. "Wow," Richard said. "Hey—could you tell him the guy on the train said 'hi' too?"

A terraced stone staircase led to a formal garden with trimmed shrubs and slender potted trees. Sunlight glinted brightly off the wide walkways. Stanislaw shaded his eyes with his hand. "Over there," he pointed, "is an arcade, very wide and quite long. Noblemen could exercise their horses there in the rain. It's a pity my father-in-law is not free today. He knows this place so well; he could tell you a lot."

"It's a hobby of his," Kasia nodded. "He knows every stone."

"Does your mother come here much?" I asked.

"No. She's too busy, even here."

Kasia's mother served on papal commissions all over the world. She and her husband met Karol Wojtyla in Kraków when he was a new priest and she was a young physician; they had worked together ever since.

"Uncle Richard!" The boys returned, panting. Charlie held out an orange. "We picked this for you! From the tree! A papal orange. Most excellent." A moment later Richard gagged and spat a mouthful of bitter pulp into a bush. The boys, howling with delight at having once again proved Uncle Richard an easy mark, bolted before he could exact revenge.

"Come," said Kasia. "I'll show you Holy Father's favorite spot."

We walked on, past ancient statues and sculpted trees until we came to a green clearing with a long, still reflecting pool. At the far end was a white marble statue of the Virgin. In front of the statue there was a simple prie-dieu. A chair was off to the side.

"He meditates here every day," said Kasia. "It is so peaceful. Usually."

"Hey!" At the edge of the pool the boys were trying to shove each other into the water. "Charlie! You're cheating!"

"I never cheat! I am intent!"

Kasia clapped her hands. "Children, why don't you show Uncle Richard the amphitheatre? You can play there for a while."

Charlie's eyes lit up. "Gladiator! I will defeat you!"

"Charlie! Let your brother up, please. Thank you."

Kasia frowned. "Now they will both need baths before dinner."

We walked on, past lemon trees and kiwi vines, Roman ruins and cow pastures ("papal cows," the boys called them). Eventually Stan led us back to the gate, and the guard once more unlocked the door for us. "Grazie," Kasia murmured. "Grazie! Grazie!" the boys roared. The guard smiled.

The Zajacs hugged us good-bye and started up the incline to the palace. The Swiss Guard saluted as Charlie tore past them. The huge wooden doors swung shut behind them, and our friends were gone.

Richard and I headed back to the train station.

On our last day in the Eternal City, Lee surprised us with tickets to a small guided tour through the "Nova Scavi" she'd scored through the embassy. Begun at the orders of Pius XII, the *Nova Scavi*, or "new excavations," began as a little publicized effort to determine really, truly, and seriously whether the body of St. Peter lies beneath the Basilica as tradition has affirmed since before Constantine built the first church on the site. The excavations are now open by arrangement to small groups of tourists. Our guide, a German graduate student, was superb both for her learning and her dramatic sense.

For an hour or so, she took us through the ancient Roman cemetery that lies beneath the church, tossing off juicy tidbits of history and archeological lore, showing us a few graves that were clearly those of first-century Christians, well-to-do Romans who had been converted within decades of Christ's death. Then quite without preparation, she ushered us to the final stop on the tour, a set of human bones in a partially cut-away tomb, and said simply, "and here, directly beneath the high altar where the pope says mass when he is at St. Peters, we see the bones of a man, about sixty years old at the time of his execution, which was done by crucifixion in the first century AD, with the curious detail that the angles of the wounds show that he was hung on the cross upside down. Beyond that, we cannot speak."

I prayed, anyway, for the same intention I had prayed for at every other church and shrine we'd been to, never telling Richard, whose hopes I feared to raise, what I was doing, and carefully concealing my plan from Lee, the brainy atheist, for fear of looking foolish. Lee is horrifyingly good at figuring things out and ridiculously well read. When we had done St. Peter's, St. John Lateran, St. Paul Outside the Walls, St. Lawrence Outside the Walls, Santa Maria Maggiore, Santa Croce in Jerusalem, and St. Sebastian Outside the Walls, I was sure she would tumble to the fact that I had designed our itinerary to cover the traditional "Seven Churches of Rome," thus turning our tourist jaunt into an actual official pilgrimage. Fortunately she never noticed. Maybe she was distracted by the old Italian guy in Santa Maria Maggiore, the first of the seven we visited, who decided Lee (a) was Italian; (b) must know his son in Cleveland (where Lee has never been); and (c) was the granddaughter he never had. He jabbered away at her about these and other subjects for more than an hour, leading her around the church linked arm in arm to show her his favorite spots and tell her the story of how Columbus's gold had come to adorn the ceiling of the magnificent church. Of course he spoke in Italian, which Lee does not speak. Being both impeccably polite and fluent in French she was able to conceal this fact from him. From then on, however, I noticed that whenever we entered a church she wore a wary and distracted look that suggested that her awesome deductive powers might not be quite at their peak.

In any event I got away with it. And as we left the Vatican that day I could tell myself I had done everything I could for my cause. Next to the Holy Land, Rome is the most important pilgrimage center in Catholic tradition. A pilgrimage honors the faith of the martyrs and expresses the pilgrim's own faith in concrete terms: here I am. I'm showing up because I believe. And because I want something.

Finally we had to go home. The in-flight movie was *My Cousin Vinny*. Now that's Italian.

III

In the confessional the priest asked me, from out of the blue, as I had not invited any counseling, "What would you say is the greatest cross in your life?"

I hesitated. "Envy?" I guessed.

"Envy is the result you feel from this cross. What is the cross?"

I sighed. I hated getting into this. "That I could never have kids."

Usually after I tell someone this there's a pause, an "Uh-oh, sorry I asked" moment. But this priest didn't miss a beat. He began with the usual "God is preparing you for something" schtick, without a breath seguing right into the "you've got to stop the pointless grieving and get on with it" schtick, blah blah blah, same old, same old.

Then he actually said something new. "You know, Christ didn't have children either."

This had never occurred to me. I just said, "Hmm."

"So?" he said, "What's the difference?"

I thought a second. "Well, for starters, I'm already older than Christ was when He died, so I have been living with it a lot longer."

The priest, who was Polish, burst out laughing. "Good point," he conceded.

ॐ • ॐ

All right. I know I can't tell this story without writing about infertility. I'm going to do it, but only under the rules. Don't think, don't judge, don't edit, don't control, let go, write what is true.

ॐ • ॐ

Early morning. A drab waiting room in a New York City hospital.

As usual no one wanted to be there. Years later I would learn about other waiting rooms, far more depressing. But these were awful in a different way, full of tension and wounded pride, shame and furtiveness.

Most of it we brought there ourselves. Yet in this, as in most of the clinics I'd been to, it seemed as if the place ratified our shame. The waiting room was really a hallway, and "waiting" meant standing on line, leaning against the wall. Once when I had tried to sit down in a real waiting room down the hall the nurse had brusquely evicted me. "You wait out there," she said, pointing me back to the line. The "examination room" at the end of our hallway was actually a passageway for the doctors. Strangers walked through casually as you lay exposed on your back, hospital gown pulled up to the waist, trying to get a look through your knees at the ultrasound screen.

ᔓ • ᔕ

Another hospital. Another waiting room. In this one we sit. As always in these places there was little conversation. Everyone had the same story and no one wanted to hear it again. But I remember two women, obviously strangers, talking about hard it was to get a cab in time to make the early morning appointments. "When I told the cabdriver I wanted to go to the hospital," one of the women said, "he said, 'You sick?' I said, 'No, I'm not sick.' 'So why you go to hospital?' So I figured what the heck, I told him I was trying to get pregnant. He was very interested. He told me all about a guy back in his village in Ghana, or wherever, who made charms for women who were trying to conceive. 'I can get for you! Always work! Always baby!'" They chuckled and fell silent. The other woman leaned forward in her folding chair. "So—did you get his number?"

ᔓ • ᔕ

Looking for a house in what we used to call "upstate" New York, now just a remote northern suburb of the city. A realtor shows me a sweet little cottage, all redone inside with a newly papered nursery. "The couple who lived here bought the house because they wanted to start a family. But she couldn't get pregnant. They're divorced now," the realtor said. I look around the pretty little nursery again. I am standing in a tomb.

ॐ • ॐ

We were married in 1981. We wanted children, but it was OK, even convenient that they did not come right away. For a year or two we barely thought about it. Then a few years passed and we progessed from not thinking about it to not talking about it. Part of it must have been that neither one of us wanted to know whose fault it was. Then about five years before that first trip to Italy, we decided, in fine American fashion, that we had a problem and it was time to solve it.

The first infertility specialist we saw had his offices in North Shore University Hospital, a big deal teaching hospital on Long Island. My brother-in-law Kevin had consulted around with his doctor friends, mostly ex-jocks from his Johns Hopkins frat. They fingered the guy I was going to see as one of the top fertility docs anywhere.

I don't think they were referring to his people skills. For my first test he tore a piece of tissue out of my womb (no anesthesia), then immediately strode out of the room without a word to me (my eyes tearing from the pain), congratulating himself out loud as he admired the curling strip of flesh on his knife. "Beautiful. Just beautiful."

He did some tests. Gave me some drugs. After a few months I went in for a consultation to see if the drugs were working. I was alone, Richard was working. As I walked into his office he had my file open on his desk. He glanced at the first page, then he slapped the folder shut and said, "If I were you I'd just give up."

I walked in shock to the parking lot. I found my car, I opened the door, I sat down behind the wheel. Then I tried to put the key in the ignition. It wouldn't go. It had always gone in before, but now I couldn't get it in. I kept jabbing away and I couldn't get the damn key into the slot.

I folded my arms on the steering wheel, put my head down, and burst into tears.

It was nearly a year before I sought a second opinion.

But of course I did. And another and another. I would read an article somewhere about some exciting new advance. I would get a list of names from somewhere, sometimes from an article, sometimes from friends, and I would call new doctors and go see them or at least try to get to see them. I remember one I called asked me who I'd seen so far, and when I told him about the guy at North Shore he said, "Well, if he couldn't help you I don't know what you expect me to do." At least he knew his limitations.

The same could not be said for another MD I saw in New York, who lied to me about what kind of procedures he performed. "I didn't say I *did* that one," he smirked, when I showed up for the consultation. "I said I *knew about* it." That'll be three hundred bucks, sucker.

There were other doctors. Too many to remember. I do recall a sweet blonde girl who averted her eyes every time she used the phrase "child-free." My favorite ever was a courtly Chinese woman of about sixty. I really was fond of her, so much so that I wrote a short story about her at the time, long since lost. An optimist, she cheerfully assured me that my only problem was volume. I can still see her, bowing from the waist as she shook my hand in farewell. "More sex, Mrs. Vigilante! More sex. Sex like river!"

Richard did the rounds too. I remember the first time he came home from a consult after a fertility test, looking puzzled. "Apparently I have plenty of sperm. The problem is they lack motivation." He had one operation; he took a fertility drug for nearly a year and endured searing headaches from it. I remember one doctor suggested the problem could be circulatory. He suggested propping up the foot of the bed on telephone books so Richard's blood would flow in the right direction. Unfortunately at that same time Richard was suffering from acid reflux, and the GI specialist had already told him to prop the head of the bed up on telephone books. So that was a wash.

Then there was the doctor whose theories all revolved around the temperature of the scrotum, which apparently should be about a degree lower than the rest of the body. (To keep them motivated? "OK, guys, I know it's chilly in here, but the quicker you find a target and get in there, the quicker you'll warm up. Now go! Go! Go!") He advocated boxer shorts, or a strategically placed damp paper towel for men who could not give up their jockeys. Or, the ultimate solution—especially for those technologically inclined "early adopters"—a mechanized combo harness and spray gun, apparently of his own invention, that, as the man went blithely about his daily business, would periodically lift the testicles and give them a discrete hosing. Great at board meetings. A blast on the subway. And you thought you had nothing to talk about at cocktail parties.

What really got us off the chilled testicles guy was the way he kept calling it "scrotal" temperature in his thick Yiddish accent. We're New Yorkers for goodness sakes. How many million times had we heard the soundtrack to *Fiddler On the Roof*? "Scrotal! She's going to marry Scrotal? But he's poor! They'll have nothing!"

Then there was Ilsa, She Wolf of the SS. Richard's testicles having been on ice for months to no effect, it was decided to take a closer look. The woman assigned to take this closer look was a fortyish, blonde, high-cheek-boned, six-foot-tall, ultrasound technician, with a thick German accent, and, as Richard never fails to mention, "enormous breasts." This test, like most infertility procedures, naturally involved Richard stripping stark naked and lying flat on his back on a freezing cold table. Nearby Ilsa prepared the tools of her trade including a gel of some sort to improve the contact between the hand-held ultrasound scanner, and, um, Richard.

Now never in any such situation, and I have been in many, has the doctor showed any hesitation to touch what ever part of me he needed to touch to get the job done. Apparently the union of six-foot, blonde, German ultrasound technicians with "enormous breasts" maintains a more exacting ethical code, because instead of just grabbing what she needed to grab and doing the darn test, Ilsa spent the next half-hour struggling to accomplish this task while making no actual physical contact with the private parts in question. Instead of smearing the gel on with her hands, for instance, she squirted it from, if not a polite distance, than certainly far enough away to affect her aim, with the result that instead of a light coating of the stuff where it belonged there were great blobs of it everywhere.

Then there came the all-important positioning of the testicles, which in the way of testicles under the influence of gravity were hanging too low for her to get a good picture. Perhaps she should just pick them up? But no, you are forgetting the voluptuous, six-foot, blonde medical technicians' ethical code.

Perhaps Richard should just pick them up?

No he is clumsy layman and his hands vill get in zee vay. Instead Ilsa instructs him to raise his knees and spread them as far as he can. She then hands him a small white hand towel, which Richard is to fashion into a sort of testicle brassiere with which to defeat gravity. This he tries in all good faith. Unfortunately what with the massive amounts of that slimy gel everywhere every time he gets some decent elevation the poor babies slip out of their bra and go flop on the table. This is not much fun. So Richard, out of a decent sense of self-protection, not to mention due consideration for his prospective progeny, tries to compromise, struggling to find an elevation adequate to Ilsa's needs, but not likely to produce another crash landing.

Ilsa is not pleased.

"Higher, please."

Richard cautiously inches them up a bit.

"Higher! They must be higher!"

Ooops, too high! Slip. Flop. Smack. Groan.

Complicating the entire procedure are those "enormous" breasts, which, given the way Ilsa is leaning over to do the exam, place a definite limit on how high Richard can go before he starts poking them in a way almost certain to be frowned upon by buxom blonde medical technicians everywhere.

"Again please! Let usz try again. Higher."

"I am trying."

"You muzst ztry harder. Higher! Higher! Zay are too low; it muzst be higher!!!!

"Higher!

"Higher!

"High!

"Heil!

"Heil! Sieg heil! Oh! Oh! Mine Führer! I am here!"

OK, I made up the "Führer" bit.

The test was inconclusive.

I took fertility drugs too; that is, I took them until the headaches became so bad I started seeing double, and my doctor told me that was a bad sign and I should stop. I took injections—Richard and I went to the specialist's office and they taught R how to shoot some stuff into my hip. In the office Richard did it perfectly, but in a classic case of leaving it in the locker room, as soon as we got home he lost his touch. Rare was the shot from Richard that was not followed by me giving him a shot of my own.

Finally one doctor said, "They made sure your tubes were open, didn't they?"

"Uh—I don't know. I don't think so."

"Hm. Maybe we should check."

We checked. They weren't.

More fun and games. Up to New Haven to have my tubes opened by means of little balloons. Drive back to

New York after the procedure, Richard pulling over to the side of the highway once or twice so I could throw up, an after-effect of the anesthesia. But at least now I could get pregnant!

I didn't.

Meanwhile, at the same time we are going through all this, the whole in vitro revolution is happening. In vitro fertiliztion. IVF. The baby maker, the magic petri dish, the source of happy young families all over the country.

IVF.

The Big Hope.

Forbidden by the Catholic Church.

OK, go ahead. I know you're dying to say it. So come on, gimme your best shot.

"A bunch of celibate priests have no business telling married people how to run their lives."

Whoa! You thought that up all by yourself. Well aren't you the quick one.

"The Catholic Church is always standing in the way of scientific progress. Galileo! Galileo!"

Please. Do we really have to go through the whole story of the world's original scientific publicity hound, again. Because I hear the real problem was the telescopes weren't selling too well until he backed some clueless cardinals into a corner and forced them to put him on trial.

Any others?

Ah, yes, how could I forget.

"You Catholics have to learn to think for yourselves. You can't just go through life being blindly obedient to Rome."

Sorry. Three strikes and you're out. Call me when you've got one I haven't heard.

I didn't want anything to do with it. Problem was, as time went on, that increasingly meant the doctors didn't want anything to do with me.

It got so I could almost time it.

YOUNG DOC: It says in your file you haven't tried in vitro yet.

ME: No, I'm not interested in in vitro.

YOUNG DOC: Gee, what's the problem?

ME: I have religious reasons.

YOUNG DOC: (Shocked expression on face, then it dawns on him, frozen little smile.) Ah. (Pause, thinks, speaks.) In that case I don't really know what I can do for you.

The above scenario was played out, with some variations, a half-dozen times. Richard once asked one of Kevin's doctor friends about it: "We're paying customers. Why would they turn us away?"

"Simple," the guy explained, "they are trying to keep their numbers up, their success rate." As unreliable as IVF was (still is) it worked a lot better than anything else. Kevin's friend even asked if I had stood on "the line" at New York Hospital. Apparently it was famous. "Why do you think they wouldn't let her sit in the waiting room? The waiting room is for IVF patients, the ones they actually want."

Worse in a way were the docs who didn't turn me away immediately. I remember one, a lovely young woman with children of her own, who wanted me to do IVF in the worst way, but promised to try other methods first. One afternoon, in another one of that long line of white cubicles, I sat weeping on the examination table after she told me that the latest treatment had failed. "There, there," she said, patting my shoulder. "It's just more ammunition for me to get you to do IVF!" I am not kidding. She wanted so much to help me have kids that she actually called my empty womb "ammunition."

In most cases, simply saying the word "Catholic" was enough. As soon as most docs heard that you could just see the mask descend, a stiff uncomfortable politeness, the only response they could make to an unfortunate faux pas, as if all of a sudden I had started telling farmer's daughter jokes.

In a way it was the easy answer. It shut them up. But I can't say it was the whole answer. I didn't do it all for God. I had a deep, gut-level revulsion against the whole idea. I could never forget Richard and the doctor batting ideas back and forth at one of our first consultations. "We could give her this. We could start her on that." We could do this to her. We could do that to her. I felt like I was at a tennis match. And I was the ball. All I could think was, *Not to me you're not, boys.*

As one friend undergoing infertility treatment put it, "You start to feel like a white rat after a while." Well, I didn't want to be a white rat. Infertility was a powerful enough assault on my womanhood. I couldn't afford to give any more ground.

And of course even the part that was about God was about me too. About my obedience and about what I wanted in return.

"Blind obedience. Blind obedience." That's what they always call it.

Well, fine. It is blind. Blind because there is so much we are always blind to. Isn't that really the point of the Fall? Even two people who walked with God in the cool of the evening, two people whose vision was not yet clouded by sin, even their obedience needed on some occasions to be blind. Even with all their special advantages there was so much they could not see, perhaps so much He could not let them see because the vision would have overwhelmed them, stripped them of their freedom, and denied them the possibility of love. Even in those clear-seeing days faith was essential to our humanity.

But that's philosophy. Is that why I obeyed, really and truly? Who am I kidding?

Why then?

Partly because by then I had learned what the alternative was. I knew that abandoning God was the route of despair. And despair was always so close in those days I couldn't risk it.

I realized something else as well. I genuinely believed in the virtue of obedience in part because obedience is one virtue I can actually attain, sometimes. It is something I can actually offer to God and know I can make good on the offer. One must bring something to the altar, after all.

I think that I did it, in the end, because when I die, and it comes my turn to be judged, whatever faults and failings, whatever sins large or small are laid to my account, at least I'll be able to say this:

"The hardest thing I ever did in my life I did for You. The world promised me what I wanted most and I turned it down, because I believed in You and Your Church, and Your Church told me 'no.' Even when everyone was telling me I was a fool to submit to You; even when I played with the babies, even a few blessed babies who had come into the world by the way You had forbidden me, babies You loved, babies You made Your children by the loving obedience of Your Son, babies I played with and loved and bought Christmas presents for—even when I didn't understand, even when I couldn't feel You anywhere, even when I hated it, I did what You asked. Despite all the sins and screw-ups and failures to be what You wanted me to be, however often

I have buried my talents in the ground, however I have failed to be fruitful for You in other ways, at least in this one thing, this one unbearable thing, I can honestly say I was obedient at great cost.

"And if that isn't enough for You, well, it's all I've got. If that's not enough, then I never had a chance with You from the beginning. You are Truth itself. And the truth about me is that this pathetic submission is the closest I could come to being like You."

I believe in obedience. But I also believe in miracles. So I began to ask for one. Over and over again. Begged for it, bargained for it, pleaded for it. The old woman harrassing the unjust judge had nothing on me. I tried everything. I applied to the designated saints for help. St. Gerard Majella, patron saint of expectant mothers and wannabes: I stayed a wannabe. St. Jude, patron of the hopeless case: apparently I was not hopeless enough. St. Anthony of Padua, finder of lost articles, Doctor of the Church and champion miracle worker: Take a hike, Signora.

The jokes are because I don't like writing about this. It's easier to write about the doctors and the scientists because they just make me mad, and maybe because in all their hubris they are the ones who look like fools. What I can't stand to write about are the prayers, the pilgrimages, and novenas and saints appealed to. Telling those stories I feel like the fool.

The Bible is full of stories of barren women who amazed everyone in the end. Some of them had endured painful humiliations: Sarah, the barren wife of Abraham, endured the scorn of her pregnant maid Hagar. Hannah wept and prayed for a child in the temple and earned a tongue-lashing from the high priest. Well I knew all about humiliation. But Sarah became the mother of Isaac, and Hannah bore Samuel and six more children after him. God rewarded their patience and their pain. What about mine?

While I waited for my miracle I watched several other women get theirs; friends who were childless for years suddenly and joyfully gave birth to beautiful, healthy babies. I went to the christenings; I bought the gifts; I lifted my glass in the toasts. I was named god-mother a bunch of times, the consolation prize for the childless, and dutifully held the babies over the font as the baptismal water was poured over their tiny fore-heads.

Eventually I couldn't take it. There came a time when I could not be happy for one more mother who was not me. I turned down the next godmother offer. My friends began to notice and stopped inviting me to the baby showers. That was a blessing, really. But I also noticed that the baby gossip would shut down if I was around, which can't have made them very happy to see me.

How could I not be happy about my friends' babies?

It's not as surprising as it sounds. It's true that envy, hating that someone else has what you want is a very ugly sin. It's so ugly that we can hardly believe it ever happens.

And I think that's right. I think true envy is pretty rare. But this wasn't envy really. It was worse.

If it had been envy it would have been only about the babies. But for women the pain of childlessness is never only about the babies. The truth is I was missing not only the child who was not there but the person I had failed to become. Infertility is not just a disappointment, like not getting a present you really wanted. It is a failure. Life may be a gift from God, but by God's own design it is also something we make. We are supposed to be co-creators. I wasn't. It was shaming and my life was already overwhelmed with failure and shame and had been for as long as I could remember.

For making babies was not the only thing I had failed to do. It was not even the only thing I had failed to do with Richard. For as long as I can remember I had thought of myself as a writer and as someone who would someday be a great writer and honored as such. Shortly before our wedding, Richard, who would go on to become a great editor and launch the careers of scads of writers, and make dozens more look better than they had any right to, told me, "I am marrying the best writer I know." He really believed it. I really believed it. We would do great things together.

III

He did. And I had four unfinished novels in my drawer, books even I didn't believe in enough to finish.

I hated my life. I hated myself. No, that's not quite right. It was not that I hated existing; it was that I seemed to myself not to exist. I was a ghost, haunting other people's lives, with none of my own. And when they asked me that worst of all questions, "who are you? why are you here?" I could think of no answer but to vanish into the mist hoping to hide my shame.

Then I met Sharon.

IV

Summer. Sometime in the late 1980s, but somehow I can't remember exactly when. In 1985 we'd come back to New York from Washington, DC, where Richard had done a brief and tumultuous stint in the Reagan White House, then worked on the *Washington Times* editorial page for a couple of years. So 1986, maybe.

I do remember that the party was held at Mickey Teeter's Fifth Avenue apartment. Mickey is a wealthy, devout Catholic woman who was trying to recruit volunteers to teach catechism classes to kids with too much money and too little family. I had no interest in teaching, but I had been invited by a mutual friend. I'd heard a lot about Mickey and I wanted to see her place, so I went.

Overlooking Central Park, laden with antique furniture and Oriental rugs, the apartment screamed "money!" But all I could look at were the floors. For the past few weeks I'd been spending every spare minute on my hands and knees scraping the hardwood floors in my grandfather's old row house in Queens, where we were living. I had wood floors on the brain. Amidst all this splendor, Mickey's floors were a horror. Parquet. Cheap looking when it had been installed and that wasn't yesterday. The varnish had to be twenty years old. What was she thinking?

"Is somebody sitting here? I can go somewhere else if anyone is." A tall, thin woman with shoulder-length curly black hair was juggling a glass of wine and a plateful of hors d'oeuvres. She eased onto the little sofa beside me. "But I just know I'm going to drop one of these little quiches on the rug if I don't sit down and I don't want Mickey to get upset. I heard she had the carpets done last month. Oh! Thanks. Mickey's kind of picky about her things. I don't blame her. She bought a lot of it in Europe, Spain, mostly, I think. Don't you just love that picture?"

Above the fireplace was a large oil portrait of our hostess reclining on a divan. She wore a flowing green gown with a cinched waist and three-quarter sleeves and diamonds around her neck. It must have been painted decades before.

"Very nice," I said.

"Oh, yeah. Mickey's gorgeous now, but she was a true beauty. She was an actress. It's such a shame about her skin." She lowered her voice. "It's the smoking."

"I see."

"Mmph." She wolfed down a handful of party food. "I'm Sharon, by the way. I've seen you around, haven't I? You're a friend of Meghan's."

"Meghan and my husband were at college together."

"Oh, right, I knew that. You're the writer, right?"

I hated that question. "Um, yeah I write. . . . So what do you do? Are you one of Mickey's teachers?"

"Yeah. I teach second graders. It's just one afternoon a week." She rolled her eyes. "The truth is I don't really know what I should be doing with my life."

"I know the feeling."

"I have to go to a meeting after this," she said suddenly. "Want to come? I think you'll like it—well, 'like' might be too strong a word. But I'm sure you'll find it interesting."

I thought, *what makes you so sure*? I said "OK."

Half an hour later I was in a church basement somewhere off Fifth listening to a woman who looked like Sophia Loren telling a roomful of people how her alcoholic husband had his secretary call her every night to say he'd been "delayed with a client."

"I don't know why I bother with a watch," she sighed, glancing at her Cartier. "The phone rings, I know it's six o'clock: cocktail hour."

"I've heard her before," Sharon whispered. "She's a doll. Nice clothes too."

One after another, they talked about the fear and sadness in their lives, about blaming themselves and everyone else too. About disappointment and heartache and their determination to stick things out because, well, there was always the chance things would get better and what else was there to do, anyway?

I sat there in shock. These people were total strangers. And every last one of them knew my life story.

When the meeting was over Sharon turned to me. "Well, what did you think?"

"I never knew I was this angry."

She gave me a big smile. "That's exactly the right place to start. Let's go get something to eat."

I followed her to one of those polished little cafés on Madison that I never had the nerve, or the income, to enter. As she tucked into the first of two desserts (for a skinny girl she had an astonishing appetite), Sharon told me a little about herself. Her family was wealthy but troubled. Her baby sister had been an alcoholic since the age of fourteen but had finally gone into rehab. ("God is so good, Sue. I mean just amazingly good.")

"I used to think my sister was my qualifier," she sighed, using the polite Al-Anon term for 'the person who sent my life spinning out of control.' "But the more I get to know about my family the more I see I have qualifiers all over the place."

She flagged a waitress. "Could we get another of these Napoleons? They are just too yummy."

To me, "You have to try one. So who's your qualifier, Sue?"

I must have looked startled because she smiled. "I've been going to Al-Anon for two years now," she said. "You get to where you can spot it a mile away. You will, too, after a while. So. Who is it?"

I hesitated. I had lots of choices. "My brother," I said finally. "He's two years older than me."

"How long has he been drinking?"

"I—I don't know."

She nodded. "We never knew about my sister either." The waitress plopped a pastry in front of her. "Oh, I just want a little taste. The rest is for you." She pushed the plate toward me. "I like this Friday meeting," she went on. "I go almost every week. You should come with me. We can go to the meeting and get dinner afterward."

Why did I say yes? How did I know that this apparently quite daffy total stranger was the person who had been missing from my life? How was it that I knew not to screw up and just once go with my luck? Hell, given how rarely my luck had shown up, how did I recognize it?

From then on Friday nights were reserved for Sharon. Every week I took the subway from Queens to Eighty-Sixth Street and walked the few blocks to her apartment. Half the time we went to Al-Anon. The other half we'd just have dinner, usually with a few of her friends.

Drifting in and out of her apartment at any given moment might be the daughter of a German mega-industrialist, or a young Spanish nobleman who spoke elegant Castilian but whose English made him sound like Mick Jagger ("it's my governess' accent, I'm afraid").

One night the guest was a Frenchwoman who, I was discreetly informed by another guest, had the fleur-de-lis "in her family." Six months later I read about her wedding in one of those "European royalty" magazines. Sharon was one of the guests.

Not all the people coming and going to Sharon's were members of deposed royal families. There were teachers and doctors and librarians, bankers and secretaries. All wanted the same thing I wanted, to be with Sharon.

If this story is going to work, I have to be able to tell you why. Why everyone wanted to be with her. Why so many people loved her. Why I loved her.

In a love story, "why" is not always so important. We understand that to some extent love is arbitrary. A fine man or a bad man may be loved by one woman and not another. We don't say, "Oh, her love was not real because I would not love that man." But in this story I think it matters. I think you have to see that we were right to love Sharon, that we loved her because she was lovable, almost I would say impossible not to love. I never met anyone who would admit to disliking her; if I had I would have thought I was in the presence of a monster.

Part of it was that loving Sharon was just so much fun. She was very smart. Phi Beta Kappa in her junior year and at Dartmouth, majoring in medieval history. Nevertheless in those years in New York she was more than a little lost in the world, or, as I would say now with the benefit of hindsight, out of context. This was a burden to her and sometimes made her sad or impatient. But because she had this wonderful combination of innocence and bluntness, determined cheerfulness and lack of inhibition, it was often very funny as well. Being part of Sharon's life often felt like being a straight man in a long-running sitcom. She would have been the innocent, lovable alien sent by her superiors to live in an earthling culture she didn't quite get.

I remember once she took one of those Johnson O'Connor tests that are supposed to help you figure out what to do with your life. One of the qualities they test for is "foresight," the ability to predict the consequences of decisions. The Johnson O'Connor lady later told Sharon she had the lowest foresight score of anyone she had ever tested. (My lowest score was for "wiggly block." We all took the test—because Sharon had.) It was probably a mistake for Sharon to tell us about her foresight score. We used it against her for months because it seemed to explain so much:

Once in therapy (we shared a therapist for a while) she decided to try some art therapy, drawing pictures of herself and her dreams. It wasn't until after she'd handed her therapist the drawings that she remembered she always drew herself naked. "Kind of embarrassing," she mumbled later.

A first date, coming to pick her up at her apartment, as usual a mess. She cleans madly, even does the laundry including piles of lingerie. (Sharon had beautiful lingerie.) Naturally she hangs the frillies in her bathroom. Guy shows up. Been in the subway for an hour. So naturally the first thing he asks . . .

Cars. I can't even begin to tell all the car stories, partly because the record of destruction and disaster had begun long before I met her. Someone, a secret enemy no doubt, had the brilliant idea of giving her a car while she was still in college. College was Dartmouth. In New Hamphire. Up North. Home of the Winter Carnival. One snowy evening, the story goes, she parked it near the top of an icy and remarkably steep hill outside the dining hall. A few minutes later the dining hall resounded with a crash and shouts of "Oh, my God!" from some girls looking out the window. In one mass the entire student body including Sharon rushed outdoors to see what could possibly have happened. Hmmmm. How strange. A car at the bottom of the hill—impaled on a pine tree.

She destroyed one car by filling its tank with regular gasoline instead of the diesel it required; she totaled another on the Taconic Parkway within an hour of getting it as a gift from her parents. Once when the car she shared with a roommate refused to start one of them got the bright idea of pouring gasoline on the carburetor; in the ensuing fortunately small explosion Sharon's eyebrows were singed off.

You might think a woman with such a record would

be better off taking a cab. Nope. For her twenty-first birthday her parents gave her a string of pearls; she left them in a cab and never saw them again. For her thirtieth birthday her parents tried again with a second string; she left that one in a cab too. This time she was so embarrassed she went out that very afternoon and bought herself a duplicate string, not an easy thing to do since the ones she'd lost had been hand-selected and hand-strung. I don't know if she ever told her parents about it.

One of Sharon's great friends was Elaine S., a woman of our mother's generation. When Elaine's husband, to whom Sharon was also very close, was dying of emphysema, Sharon was relentless in rounding up prayers for his soul. Returning late from Elaine's one evening, she turned into her garage on Ninety-Third Street and parked in her usual space. As she climbed out of her car she spotted the parking attendant, an elderly black man who always seemed to be there keeping an eye on things. Aha!

The man stood up as she approached. Sharon got right to the point. "Are you a praying man?" she demanded.

He eyed her calmly. "Yes, ma'am," he replied in a soft Southern drawl. "I most certainly am. I pray every time I see you go in and out of this garage."

I loved, loved, loved Sharon's religious faith. And I was jealous of it.

Sharon had The Real Thing. Her faith was not some painstakingly acquired overlay, but the natural center of her life. Listening to her talk about Christ was a completely new experience for me. She thought Jesus was fascinating. She loved Him, sure. But more than that, she liked Him. She wanted to be with Him. "I like Our Lord so much, and He's so interesting," she wrote me once. No one had ever described Christ—not the guy in the stories of the gospels but the one in her heart—as "interesting" before. I still wonder what she meant.

Sharon did not proselytize. But she radiated faith. Getting to know Sharon you got to know faith as essential to life as breathing and just as natural. She was not preachy but she was forthright and her moral sense was contagious. One night while she was still at Dartmouth she went on a date with a young man she had just met. He kissed her on the lips. Sharon was, as she put it, "morally outraged." She went back to her dorm and told a roommate about it, "and by the time I was done with the story she was just as morally outraged as I was!" She was laughing at herself as she told me the story, but I wish I could have heard that conversation.

One night while I was writing this book Richard and I had dinner with a great friend of ours, a famous writer and one of the few I know who really deserves the label "genius." He asked me about my writing, a subject he has absolutely no compunction about prying into. I told him that I was writing about Italy, and that a lot of different characters came into the story, among them my old friend Sharon. This man had met Sharon exactly once at a hastily assembled dinner party at our house in Queens years before. But the mention of her name got his full attention. "If you can capture her on paper that will be a real achievement."

そ • ゐ

"Inspiration," an infusion of the spirit.

Spiritus, breath or wind.

Pentecost, the "descent of the Holy Spirit upon the Apostles." A sound like a great rushing wind, and suddenly Peter, the apostle who could never keep his foot out of his mouth, becomes a dazzling witness, an oratorical genius making himself understood by every member of a multilingual crowd.

The spirit as wind always makes me think of Sharon. Refreshing but also rearranging. No foresight? Isn't that what inspiration feels like? Sudden and surprising and not pausing to work out the consequences. That comes later.

We say prophets see the future. But wasn't it just the opposite with the real prophets? Wasn't foresight just the thing they lacked, these men who spoke the truth without consciousness or care for the consequences? Even the Old Testament prophecies that most sound like predictions, like Isaiah's foretelling of Christ, burst forth from the seer like a light that blinds as much as it reveals. I wonder how St. Francis, whose life after his conversion consisted almost entirely of ignoring the consequences of his actions, would have done on the Johnson O'Connor test?

ⅎ • ℜ

Loving Sharon was a blast. But what was it like to be loved by her?

"How is your book coming along?" Elaine asked one evening when a clutch of us was gathered, as we often were, at her beautiful Westchester home. Elaine is lovely and the question was kindly meant. But it was my least favorite question in the world. There are few things more embarrassing than being an unsuccessful writer. You work hard, you write every day, you send out queries and samples, yet it looks to all the world as if you do nothing at all. You attend no meetings, you bring home no paychecks, none of the things real working people do. During those years I had nothing concrete to testify to my struggle, not even a failed book to point to and say, "I did that." Every time the subject of work came up I felt like a fool, or a liar. I was making a career of being ashamed.

Why not just drop it?

I had tried. I had worked at a dozen jobs—in law

firms, in shops, in lobbying offices, and public relations firms. I learned a lot in those jobs, chiefly that I was no good at any of them. I also learned that when I did not write I became even more depressed, more irritable, and more unpleasant to be around than I normally am. I learned I needed to write to feel like I had a place where I belonged in the universe. Possibly that need says something very bad about me. More than likely the need to find my identity in my work is evidence of some pathetic personality disorder, another excuse to be unhappy, one more horrible self-deception. Maybe finding myself on the *New York Times* best-seller list would not change anything. I would not be the least bit surprised. So my need to write is pathetic and embarrassing. So what else is new?

Was I feeling particularly bad about my alleged career that night? Had something especially discouraging happened that week? Or was it this bad all the time? I don't know, but when Elaine brought it up I could feel myself shrinking into the chair.

"Well," I said, "I, well, you know. I'm still working on it."

She let it go at that.

Sharon was leaving for a vacation the next day, and I would not see her for two weeks. "Let me drive you home," she offered. "There's something I want to talk to you about."

Heading south from Elaine's Westchester home we

saw an accident. "Poor guy. Let's pray for him. Hail Mary, full of grace . . ."

"Could you pray with your eyes open, please?"

"Sorry." She finished her Hail Mary and hit a pothole. "Do you mind if we stop by my place for a minute? I have to pick something up. I'll take you right home, I promise."

Sharon's apartment was strewn with enough clothes and suitcases for a year's safari. It was always like this before she left on a trip: total chaos. Between the inherent conflict between poor foresight and packing, and the endless list of phone calls she was always trying to return before going, it was a wonder she ever managed to leave New York.

She picked her way through the debris and poured us some sherry.

"You didn't like Elaine asking about your book?"

"No."

"You should have seen yourself. You just shrank. Don't do that. You're already a petite; there's nowhere else to go."

"Ha, ha."

"I'm serious. I understand. I grew up the same way. I know what the constant criticism does. We become our own worst enemies. Cutting ourselves off before we've given ourselves a decent chance. I read your article."

I had done a piece on our infertility saga for an

extremely obscure journal. I had no idea anyone had seen it.

"It was beautiful, Sue. It was honest and real and brave."

"Well, thanks."

"It's your calling. Don't let anyone talk you out of it."

I sat on the couch, unable to speak, torn every which way by love and shame, joy at knowing Sharon and profound regret that I was only me.

No foresight? Perhaps. But love knows. Abruptly the lecture ended. "Let's try on some scarves." For the next half hour we went through Sharon's vast collection, tried on dozens, cheered or booed colors. She showed me some new knots. Finally she dug into a drawer and pulled out one I hadn't seen, still wrapped in tissue. "I just wanted to give you this before I left. I don't know what I was thinking buying it. Not my colors at all. I don't know why I've held onto it for so long—unless it was because I was keeping it for you!"

"It's beautiful," I said, turning the scarf over in my hands. Silk. Soft sage green, subdued gold accents.

"It's a Gucci—knockoff! It will be beautiful on you. Here, let me show you."

Later I asked my therapist, "Is that what mothers do?"

How could I of all people be this lucky? Drifting

through my cold, dark universe, what had brought me into the orbit of this Sun, suddenly and unexpectedly warming me through and through with the unconditional love I had heard rumor of and had been sure was a lie?

She left me at the curb in front of my house. "I can't come in. I have to finish packing. Don't skip Al-Anon while I'm gone. Don't stop writing either. It's all going to work out, Sue. It's all going to come together one day. Finish your book. And say a prayer I don't break a leg on the slopes!" And she drove off, zipping confidently the wrong way down our one-way street.

V

One morning I woke up and I knew she was going.

I had been unable to reach her for several days. That in itself was not unusual; Sharon's social calendar was always jam-packed, and she was often impossible to get hold of. How did I know? Don't ask me. How do lovers know?

That evening Richard and I were to attend a book party at the Forbes building on lower Fifth Avenue. I had arranged to stop by Sharon's apartment on East Eighty-Ninth in the afternoon and visit for a while. When I got there Sharon was dressed to go out; she had an appointment that evening, too, and had gotten ready early. She wasted no time. "Let's go over to the Sherry-Netherland. I have something to tell you that's going to require alcohol."

My heart sank. "OK," I said. Then I started talking. About anything. I wouldn't let myself think about why I wouldn't shut up, but I knew what I was doing: I had to keep Sharon from getting a word in edgewise, or she would tell me.

So then I said, "Well, Meghan, if you're going to the

museum later maybe I could meet you there and . . . ," I gabbled on in sheer panic.

She paid no attention. She murmured an occasional "mm-hmm," but I could see she was not merely ignoring me: she was keeping her focus on her plan, already screening out any objections or attempts to dissuade her. She looked straight ahead, her eyes sharp with determination. My heart sank even farther and my tongue worked even faster. "By the way, Sharon, did Meghan tell you that Cindy and Ruth are going to . . ."

It was a warm day in early spring, the kind of day that makes the heads of winter-weary New Yorkers spin with relief and recklessness. The banks of cut flowers in front of the Korean groceries, which in winter have a kind of fragile, ornamental appearance seemed to be breathing again, sending their fragrance wafting out over the sidewalk and giving passing pedestrians surprising romantic ideas. On the streets of the city the first outdoor cafés were making their appearance with a few tables scattered just off the sidewalks, looking tentative as if resurgent winter might chase them back inside at any moment.

The bar in the Sherry-Netherland was one of Sharon's favorite hangouts. We sat down at a table and she flagged a waiter. I don't remember what she ordered; I ordered a Sea Breeze. When the drinks arrived I asked the waiter to bring me another right away. Sharon did not look surprised. "Do you want something to eat with that?" she asked.

"No," I shook my head. "But I know what you're going to tell me, and I know I'm going to need another drink."

"OK." Sharon picked up her glass with a kind of "here goes" look on her face and said, "I am going to Mississippi to join the Sisters of St. Paul the Evangelist."

"I know." I couldn't look at her. "I know you are." I could feel my throat tightening. I picked up my Sea Breeze and gulped half of it down.

"Don't you want to say something?" my friend asked gently.

"No. No, I don't. I don't want to talk about it. If I do I'll cry and I don't want to do that on Fifth Avenue, OK?"

"OK." Sharon nodded. "OK."

Sharon had casually considered religious life off and on since college, but for most of the years I knew her in New York she struggled trying to find her place in the world rather than out of it.

She had a busy life. Her calendar was packed with appointments and fundraisers; she was on the boards of I don't know how many charitable foundations; she had dinner dates booked months in advance, countless friends and God knows how many out-of-town weekends skiing or sailing or foxhunting. But she felt a nagging emptiness at the center, an unsettling sense that life was slipping past, and she still didn't know what she was supposed to be doing.

For years she thought the trouble was she had not found the right career. The trouble was she didn't feel one calling to her, and those she did try had a tendency to blow up in her face. She taught Spanish in a small Catholic girls' school, an experience she described as "a Charlie Chaplin movie, run backwards." For a while she ran a literacy foundation in New York of which her father was the chief supporter, but it never interested her.

She wanted to do something for God, but she wasn't sure what. For a while she was deeply interested in Natural Family Planning. She got some training and learned all about temperature charts and mucus analysis. Finally confident she knew all there was to know about ovulation, she got in touch with several couples, mostly newlywed friends who were interested in NFP, and invited them all to her apartment. Her idea was to teach them about NFP over dinner. The impracticality of this plan did not occur to her until the salad had been served, when she suddenly heard herself describing the various textures of vaginal mucus to people who were trying to eat. "It was just impossible. Something about the vinaigrette," she sighed. A few months later she got a note from a woman who had come to the dinner, written down everything she'd said, and that night became pregnant with twins.

V

She decided she would give teaching one more try.

She started out with the best of intentions. She spent a year in Chicago, as an assistant teacher at an experimental school. When she returned to New York she took a job at a threadbare parochial school in the Bronx.

It wasn't long before things began to unravel. The kids were unruly and unmotivated, and Sharon discovered, to her shock and horror, that she was not a particularly patient woman. She ranted, the kids acted out. One of her students gave her head lice. Soon the alpha boys were openly defying her. Night after night she came home in tears of frustration and humiliation. One day a school official spent hours in her classroom, evaluating her performance. At one point with the entire class on the brink of open rebellion Sharon, in desperate need of a diversion, darted to the wall, flipped all the switches down, and shouted, "the lights are out, the lights are out." The evaluator duly noted it all in his report.

She resigned her teaching position in June. That summer she soothed her ravaged ego in characteristic fashion by flying to Europe for a combined religious pilgrimage and continental shopping spree. After nearly two months abroad she came back, laden with cartons of designer clothes and objets d'art and suspiciously quiet.

I picked her up at the airport the day she returned. Although it was a broiling hot day in New York, it had been cool in Geneva, and Sharon was dressed accordingly. She wore a long-sleeved white linen blouse and a navy linen skirt, and her dark hair was caught back with a navy ribbon. She told me she had been hit on by two Hasidim during the flight. "I think it was because I was reading an Old Testament," she said. I said I was pretty sure it was the long sleeves.

As we headed for the Queens Midtown Tunnel she talked about Fatima. "One thing it made me see," she said, "is that time is short. I don't mean the end of the world. I mean life is short; it matters what you do with every minute of it. You only have so much time to do good. And there's so much good to be done . . . ," her voice trailed off wistfully.

After that she started investigating women's religious orders all over the country. She wrote letters, made inquiries, visited a handful of orders. She looked at a kind of social-worker order in New York State but decided social work was not her talent, and, besides, they wore the ugliest shade of slate blue she'd ever seen. She checked out the Missionaries of Charity, who had a convent in New York, but she concluded that the kind of heroic sacrifices those women make—sleeping on floors, cold-water washes, working every day with the most down-and-out characters in New York— were for, well, heroes.

She went down to Alabama to give the Poor Clares a try, but the mother superior, Mother Angelica of TV semi-fame, spent only a few minutes with her before saying, "You know, honey, I just don't think the cloister is your style."

"Oh, *Mother*!" Sharon burst out in a flood of relief, "I am *so* glad you said that because *honestly* I didn't think I'd be able to observe silence for a *minute* let alone for *hours* and I just couldn't *imagine* . . ."

I had been "following the situation closely," as they say in DC when they don't want to say, "Yes, we did wake the president to tell him the news, but he's as clueless as ever," but I was never really worried. I couldn't see Sharon giving up her friends, her designer clothes, her European vacations, her foxhunting, and her café lifestyle to live a life of poverty and routine. So I would listen to her reports and laugh as she recounted her latest string of vocational disasters, and I told myself this one most devastating of disasters, that she should succeed, would never come to pass. I might fail at everything else, but I would hold on to Sharon.

಼ • ಣ

I hated it. And I hated hating it. I loved her. I wanted to want what was best for her. And despite all the jokes about how she wouldn't last a week without her cafés, her treble-booked social calendar, and her clothes (brown, the Sister Servants' habit was brown! Sharon wearing brown—near her face! Arrrrgggghhhhh!), I knew this was right for her. Suddenly she was in context. For years for so many of us, she had been the focus. But now she would get to focus. Now she could be in love.

Didn't matter. I hated it anyway. And why not? All the important changes in my life since I returned to New York had in one way or another been possible because of Sharon. She had dragged me to my first Al-Anon meeting, my first pedicure, my first bikini wax; she had insisted I have my "colors done" (a more devoted disciple of "Color Me Beautiful" than Sharon cannot be found on planet Earth); she taught me how to tie scarves and shop for antique furniture. Most important she had taught me that the grim, stiff-upper-lip attitude I had had toward life for as long as I could remember was not something I was obliged to keep.

In the years Sharon and I were friends in New York I failed at virtually everything I attempted. I failed to get published, I failed to keep a job, I failed to get pregnant. I couldn't make money, I couldn't make babies, I couldn't make any of my youthful dreams come true. I felt deeply ashamed of my whole life. I wanted to hide in a closet and never come out.

All the while Sharon kept telling me that none of that mattered, that no one's worth comes from accomplishments, that human beings are precious in, of, and for themselves. With a lot of struggle I gradually came to realize she was telling me the truth. I did not stop trying to get published, get pregnant, etc. And the pain of failure did not go away. But there is a difference between being in pain and hating your life.

V

No one had ever permitted me to fail before Sharon. And now she was abandoning me.

I wasn't surprised. I knew perfectly well why God would want her all to Himself.

But I wanted her too. And it made me feel like a three-year-old throwing a tantrum screaming, "Mine! Mine! Mine!"

I talked to my confessor about it one day. "I just don't understand," I whined. "I know I should be glad Sharon's found what she really wants to do, but I'm not. I can't help it. I feel—I feel betrayed. And I'm . . . ," I hestitated. "I'm really, really mad at God."

He nodded. "Of course you are," he said gently. "He hasn't given you any babies, and now He's taking away your best friend. I'd be mad at Him too."

VI

From the moment word got around right up until she left, Sharon's apartment was like the smoking room at a funeral parlor. "Everything but the body," she commented wryly. It was always full of people with a stricken look on their faces. Half of them were trying to talk her out of becoming a nun. The other half were trying not to do that but couldn't help themselves.

"You'll never make it."

"You'll be bored out of your mind."

"I give you until Easter."

"Until Christmas."

"Stay here."

"Go to Europe."

"Marry me." (Even before the announcement Sharon, not a beautiful woman, had gotten more proposals of marriage than any three women I knew.)

I remember Kasia trying to talk some sense to her. "OK, join a convent, but why Mississippi? There are great orders here. What about the Dominicans?"

Sharon glared. "They *teach*!"

"Jackson is not the middle of nowhere," Meghan

said firmly. "It has an airport. We'll be able to go see her." Meghan was a convert and consequently full of certainty.

Sharon was undeterred. She set about her preparations in typical gung-ho fashion, giving away her clothes and sending her furniture into storage for her relatives to argue over.

Apparently sending an heiress with large and complicated family ties off to take a vow of poverty that may or may not turn out to be temporary is a pretty complicated thing. I think there are law firms that specialize. As always with Sharon, the real adventure lay in acquiring her wardrobe.

This should not have been a complicated process. The list of items she was expected to bring with her for her six-month tryout as a postulant was not long. A brown jumper, a couple of white blouses, some underwear, a pair of shoes, sandals, and a raincoat. The convent would supply her veil.

The sight of this short and uninspiring list, not to mention the sight of the word "brown"—Sharon is a "Winter": basic black, navy blue, true reds, but never, never, never brown—sent nearly as powerful a shock through Sharon as her announcement had done to her friends. "Oh, my God," she whispered as her eyes scanned the page a second, a third time in disbelief. Finally she looked up. "All I can say is God better exist."

But where to shop? Bloomingdale's did not have brown bib-style jumpers in stock that season. And what about this item, the "petticoat"? "Six inches below the knee, cotton or cotton-blend in A-line style"? Victoria's Secret was not going to be much help.

The biggest hurdle was the jumper. She must have tried a dozen shops and catalogues before she gave up and called the convent. A postulant picked up the phone. "I'm not surprised you can't find one; my mother ended up making mine. Do you sew?"

"Um, no . . ."

"Do you know anyone who does? Because I can send you one of my jumpers; you need two, you know. There's no real pattern but maybe someone could copy it for you."

Relieved, Sharon said it would be very kind if the girl sent her the jumper. Her relief turned to horror when it arrived. An ugly, boxy thing that looked like a reject from a stage production of *Jane Eyre*. Sharon took it to our friend Pip, who had agreed to sew a copy for her. "I can't wear this. I just can't. There must be something you can do!"

Pip eyed the dress dubiously. "Hmm . . ." She slipped into the deep, thoughtful silence characteristic of women who sew, sizing up a new challenge. She plucked at the folds of cloth that hung loosely around Sharon's waist. "I can take it in a little here. Maybe I can taper the skirt a bit . . ."

"Anything," Sharon pleaded. "Anything would be better than this."

So two jumpers were made that did not exactly fit the convent standard. We all agreed it was a small price to pay for a new vocation. Pip also made the petticoats, adding, at Sharon's request, a series of non-regulation ruffles at the hem.

A simpler item was the raincoat. At least it sounded simpler. The convent's list called for a tan raincoat with a zip-out lining. Sharon shopped for a full day before finding what she wanted, and she wore it home in triumph. "I really didn't think I was going to have any luck at all," she confided that evening. "I tried Bergdorf's, I tried Saks, but you know the minute I walked into Burberry what was the first thing I saw? There it was on the mannequin, and it was even in my size!"

"Burberry?" I repeated. "Isn't that, a little, um, pricey?"

"Well, it's not like I bought a lot of stuff there. Just the coat. So I didn't really spend that much."

I looked at the price tag. "But, Sharon . . . ," I hesitated. How to put this? "What I mean is, well, won't the nuns think it's a little odd if you show up with a five hundred dollar raincoat?"

Sharon looked puzzled. "You don't understand. This coat has to last me the rest of my life!"

The one wardrobe item she refused to have anything to do with were the sandals. She was supposed to bring a pair of Birkenstock sandals, but one look at them in a shoe store window and she rebelled. There were limits, she said. "I'll just say I couldn't find them anywhere."

I saw Sharon in her postulant garb only once, later that year when she came up to visit family. It was midsummer and New York was in the throes of an extended heat wave. I was ill, stuck in a hospital bed on Long Island the day she drove out to see me. When she arrived, hours late of course, she was wearing her "custom" jumper and what she called her "nun shoes" over a pair of knee-high wool socks. It was over ninety outside and it must have been even hotter in Mississippi. "Maybe you should just get the sandals," I said.

She stood her ground. "I'd rather die."

If there are any men reading this, I am just not sure they will get it about the clothes. One man I know who did was my spiritual director, Fr. James Halligan, the one man I have known in this life who I am sure is a saint. Fr. Halligan was chaplain to an order of nuns for years. He told me once while all the wardrobe drama was going on that people should never underestimate how much of a sacrifice it is for religious women to give up their clothes. He told me he'd known nuns, "great sisters, very holy," who dreamed about their clothes for decades after taking the veil. And years later Sharon wrote me that she had dreamed all night about one of her favorite cocktail dresses: about going to her closet, taking it off the hanger, slipping the dress on, feeling the cool slide of the silk against her skin, admiring how perfectly the color complemented her skin tone. . . . Then her alarm went off; she threw on her habit and joined the community in chapel for early mass. The gospel was from the sixteenth chapter of Matthew: "Lay not up for yourselves treasures upon earth, where moth and rust doth corrupt, and where thieves break in and steal; but lay up for yourselves treasures in heaven."

"God doesn't miss a beat, does He?" she wrote.

᠑ • ᠒

"Don't worry so much," she kept saying. "It's not going to be the way it used to be. You have a lot of tools now you didn't have before. You have me—I can still write letters, you know. I already checked about that—you have Kasia, you have Al-Anon, you have God, Sue. Remember that. I know you still feel like you're seeking, but trust me, you're on the right path now. No more detours. You're headed the right way. We both are."

The day she left I saw her off at the airport. She came tearing in to the lounge about five minutes before takeoff, with one small suitcase and her new raincoat flapping open around her. Underneath the coat she was wearing a rose pink silk dress and black patent-leather pumps with stiletto heels. "Last hurrah," she said with a grin. "Thanks for coming. I'm so sorry I'm late; I thought we might have a chance to talk but you know how it is. . . . I brought you something. She reached into her pocket and produced a postcard. "It's just a picture, but I wanted you to have it."

A glossy photograph. Stefano Maderno's effigy of the martyred Saint Cecelia. I studied the white marble figure lying on its side, the face turned away, the head clearly severed from the body, wondering if maybe I was missing something. "A—a dead person?"

"What?" She snatched the card back. "Oh, God. That's the wrong one!" She reached into another pocket and produced a different card, a nineteenth-century painting of the Virgin Mary done up like an Italian peasant woman with a kerchief and earrings, holding a plump Baby Jesus in her arms. Sharon put her finger on the child. "That's you. She's holding you, Sue. Remember, OK?" She gave me a final hug and ran for her plane.

PART II
Kasia

VII

One evening at Sharon's apartment, just months after we had met, Sharon steered me over to the sofa where a woman was sitting by herself. "I want you to meet Kasia," she said firmly. "She's a lot like you. She's very shy at first, but once you get to know her she's a riot."

Kasia gave me a timid smile and leaned forward to shake hands. She murmured something I assumed was "nice to meet you," though I couldn't be sure through the accent. "Sharon tells me you write," she said.

I felt the old pang in my chest. Time for an evasive maneuver? No. Not on Sharon's turf. No lying here. "I've been writing all my life. I'm not famous or anything. I'm not a success. I've written three books but I never found a publisher."

"And why was that?" she asked politely.

"The books weren't very good."

She winced. "Honesty," she said. Then she smiled. "A difficult quality."

"And what about you?"

Kasia had been a doctor back in Poland but she could

not practice in the U.S. without going back to medical school, which was out of the question. I made sympathetic noises. She shrugged.

"I never wanted to be a doctor."

"Then why?"

"If you don't have a profession in Poland you work in a shop. And there's nothing in the shops. You waste your life, you see. And my mother is a doctor and she wanted it of course."

"What did you want to do?" I asked.

Kasia blushed and looked away. "I wanted to be an artist." She lowered her voice. "And my mother wanted to be a writer!"

I laughed.

"*Su*-san! *Kasia*! It's about *time* you two met!"

A quite beautiful blonde woman barged onto the couch and planted herself between us. Meghan was one of my husband's oldest friends, a college chum, raised more or less pagan, and a brand new convert to Catholicism. You've heard maybe of the zeal of the convert. Meghan had it. It was knowing Meghan that had convinced me that all new converts should be snatched from the streets and swept off to the wilderness for Convert Boot Camp. There they could spend a few weeks hiking, foraging, building huts in the woods, fending off wild animals, learning basic mushroom identification, anything to wear them out until they calmed down. Once they'd been rehabilitated they could be returned to civilization, still Catholic but no longer dangerous to themselves or others.

"Sue, can you just imagine growing up with the Holy Father?"

"What?"

"Didn't she tell you? Kasia knows the pope! Of course he wasn't the pope the whole time she knew him; she knew him back in Poland. Kasia, you have *got* to tell her."

For a moment Kasia looked ill at ease. Finally she said, "He and my mother are good friends."

"But you know him, too," Meghan insisted. "She spent a lot of time with him when she was growing up. He presided at her wedding, you know." She lowered her voice to a stage whisper. "They had to smuggle her wedding dress into the Vatican!"

Now Kasia looked embarrassed. "Photographers," she explained.

"Well, I think you should tell everyone about it," Meghan declared. "People would love to hear more about the pope. I went to mass this morning and the priest was talking about the pope. And I thought 'if he only knew Kasia he'd have a lot more to say' and then I thought 'well maybe I should introduce them,' although I've never really met this priest before, but I'm sure he'd be interested in meeting Kasia and maybe her mother, too, next time she's in the United States. Has she told you about her mother, Sue?"

"The doctor . . ."

"She was in a concentration camp!"

I glanced at Kasia. She was staring fixedly at the floor.

"Yes. A concentration camp. What was it called again, Kasia?"

"Ravensbrück," Kasia murmured.

"So how's everybody doing?" Sharon brandished a bottle of cabernet. "My father sent me a case of this stuff. It's good!" She handed me a glass and refilled Kasia's. "Before I forget, Meghan," Sharon interjected smoothly, "I have those books you wanted to borrow. You can take them home tonight if you'd like."

"Oh, thanks. Have you looked at Sharon's bookcases, Sue? She has the most wonderful books about Our Lady. She has everything about Medjugorje. Do you know about Medjugorje?"

"It's in Yugoslavia," Kasia said. "They say the Virgin is appearing there. I haven't been, so I don't know."

"Yes! You know there have also been reports of apparitions in Japan and Africa and someplace in South America. And I was just reading about a visionary in Alabama who says Our Lady is asking everyone to meditate on the Passion every day. She said she was sad about there being so much sin in the world but that she was very happy . . ."

"To be in America," Kasia intoned.

Sharon had a sudden coughing fit. "I'll be right back,"

she sputtered.

Kasia winked at me.

ఐ • ౧

And you know me, Sue. I always want things to
go my own way. In religious life one has to give
up one's own way to confront this life and live it
fully and serenely. This is hard and I don't succeed much! But I'm giving it my all and I look
forward to every new day.

Love,

Sharon (Sister Stephen Marie!)

"She sounds happy," Kasia murmured.

I folded the letter. "Have you heard from her
lately?"

"She sent me a card when my mother was visiting,"
Kasia smiled wryly. "She said she assumed I needed the
encouragement."

Convent rules allowed Sharon to write each of her
friends once a month. Considering her roster of friends
this could have taken up her every free moment. Still
she was pretty good about it and sharing her letters out
loud became one of our favorite things to do.

One letter I had kept to myself: almost a year after
Sharon had gone away my bother had died of acute
complications of alcoholism. I visited him in the hospital

a few days before he died. At first I thought I was in the wrong room. I stared at an unconscious old man, with white hair, parched lips, and wrinkled green skin. I began backing out of the room, embarrassed at intruding. Beside him on the bed sat a young blonde woman, pretty in an outer-boroughs way, like a *Sopranos* character except years before *The Sopranos*. She asked kindly, "Are you looking for Gene?" She pointed to the old man. "This is Gene." He was thirty-six years old. Sharon wrote me a beautiful letter saying how sorry she was that she could not be with me.

When Sharon had finished her postulancy and taken her first vows, Kasia had gone to the clothing ceremony, when the mother superior gave Sharon, now Sister Stephen Marie, her new habit. "It was really very beautiful," she said. "Of course Sharon's mother cried the whole time. Her father didn't look pleased either, but that's to be expected; he never wanted her to go. But Sharon was simply radiant. I have never seen her so happy, so serene. The longer she's there the more she seems like her true self. Don't you agree?"

I smiled. I missed the clothing ceremony, but Sharon had written me about it. The letter ended with "Kasia looked wonderful but she was wearing a suit that was *sooo* not her color. She said she got an amazing deal at the consignment shop, but still. When you get a chance see if you can talk her into giving it to Meghan or somebody. And tell her to get some earrings!"

"Yes," I said. "I agree."

"Sharon's circle" dissolved with her departure. No surprise and no great loss. How many times can you air-kiss the same defunct European royalty before it gets old? In the two years that had passed since Sharon had left for the convent I had grown steadily closer to Kasia. Friday nights at Sharon's were replaced with pizza at the Zajacs. Richard joined us sometimes and what had been girls' night out evolved into a family friendship. The Zajacs were plugged into a whole network of Polish émigrés in New York, a circle of friends almost the polar opposite of Sharon's circle: all poor and all married and not surprisingly, given Stan and Kasia's background, all well-educated, all smart. A party with "the Poles," and they gave lots of parties, was heaven for Richard: for once he was neither the poorest nor the smartest guy in the room. He always had to be dragged away, one of the last to abandon the philosphers' circle.

The Zajacs lived in the Bronx. Stan was a graduate student in economics and had just begun writing his dissertation. They had two young sons, Walter, who was born in Poland, and Charlie, who was born shortly after they arrived in the United States.

The four of them lived in a tiny two-room apartment not far from the Fordham campus. It was crammed with books and statues and photographs of John Paul II. There was one of Walter as a two-year-old, showing the pope how to dry his hands with a towel. (The pope was paying careful attention.) Pictures of Kasia with the pope, pictures of her parents with him. JP II was everywhere.

The rest of the walls were covered with pictures by the kids. Walter's drawings were in the usual little-boy line, a lot of dinosaurs and superheroes. Charlie's superheroes were all taken from Wagner:

"This is Siegfried in the underworld. . . . Here he is with his sword. . . . Here is the Goddess Fricka. She is a witch, as you can see. . . . Here is Wotan. Why he married Fricka, I do not know."

Childless couples are like those atoms with a missing electron, or one too many electrons, or whatever. Ions, I think. The empty slot gives them a powerful proclivity to bond: with their pets (we treated our Labs like kids), certainly with their nieces and nephews, and if there aren't enough nieces and nephews around they adopt some. Richard may have a dozen godchildren; I have fewer only because I started turning them down when the infertility struggle got too painful.

I think, though, that we might have been drawn to the Zajac boys even if we had children of our own. Richard especially was drawn to Walter, a handsome, shy, quiet boy, tall and blond like his father. Very bright, sweet tempered but like all the family impish and full of jokes. (That came from Kasia, whose sense of humor was devilish.)

One of the most remarkable things about Walter was how well he dealt with being Charlie's older brother. Not an easy task, for Charlie, perhaps only four when we met him, was already a rock star of a child.

Though Charlie Zajac was born in America he was baptized by the pope one summer morning in Castel Gandolfo. Sharon was his godmother, although she very nearly wasn't. Driving to Castel Gandolfo that morning from Rome she got a late start and then got lost somewhere on the Appian Way. Stan and Kasia were naturally a little embarrassed—it's not often people keep the Supreme Pontiff waiting—but they managed to delay the ceremony a while. They were just beginning to think "proxy" when there was a fearsome screeching of tires in the courtyard. That is not a sound one expects to hear. Not only is the entrance to the courtyard guarded by the Swiss Guard, just a few steps away in the town square stands a small squad of Italian Carabineri with machine guns on their hips, to discourage, oh, say, car bombers, who might come, you know, screeching into the driveway. Sharon had come tearing up the hill, across the piazza and straight into the palace courtyard, which she definitely should not have been able to do. Imagine the Swiss Guards' surprise. I don't know how she managed to avoid getting at least tackled by one of them (not a bad fate, actually), not to mention skewered on a twelve-foot pike. Instead they let her into the palace, and she held baby

Charlie in her arms as the pope poured the water over his forehead.

Can a four-year-old be charismatic? If charisma is a deep confidence that what you care about and believe in the world will also care about and believe in, a natural assumption of leadership, backed by the skill and savvy to pull it off, then even as a small child Charlie was charismatic. A gifted athelete, as a toddler he was known as "Baby Bam Bam," his passion and quite surprising strength turning him into a one-infant wrecking force.

Loud, incredibly energetic, and fearfully tantrum-prone, two-year-old Charlie struck fear in the hearts of many. Staffers in Elaine's office used to hide when they saw Kasia coming with the baby. I have no doubt Kasia occasionally wished she could hide with them.

Somewhere between the ages of two and three Charlie passed through the phase in which tearing off one's clothes and racing out the door with an adult in hot pursuit represents the height of wit. Charlie excelled at this activity. He was still in this phase when his family returned to Castel Gandolfo one summer. Stan decided it was time for a serious talk. Fun is fun, he said, but this was not the Bronx. "While we are here, Charlie," he lectured, "you must not run outside naked. No, no, no!" he said, holding up an admonishing finger. "No running around naked! No, no, no! Understand?"

The lecture must have made a deep impression on Charlie, who from that moment became the apostle to the insufficiently clad. He took it as his mission in life to spread the word that the run-away-naked gag could only lead to perdition. But what would be the most effective way to get his message across?

Ah! Convert the leaders, and the common folk will follow.

"Holy Uncle! Holy Uncle!"

The pope stooped down to listen.

"Holy Uncle, while you are here, you must not run outside naked. No, no, no!" he intoned, shaking a tiny finger. "Do not go outside naked! Understand?"

The pope said he understood and agreed to abide by the rule.

The first time Richard joined me in a visit to the Zajacs, Charlie, maybe four at the time, greeted us by immediately and wordlessly retreating into the bedroom he shared with Walter, emerging a minute later dressed top to toe as some operatic hero, Siegfried, I think. Facing the small crowd in the living room, he bowed, then wordlessly retreated into his room. A minute later, Wotan. Then on and on, through maybe ten well-conceived costume changes, all without saying a word.

That a child his age should know his opera was perhaps not as surprising as it seems. He was raised by educated Poles and educated Poles are among the best-educated people in the world. What was astonishing was his absolute confidence that we would be as transfixed by his performance as we were.

Athletic. Passionate. Full of conviction. A flair for the stage. Who could not be reminded of the man who baptized him and wonder what the future might hold?

As Charlie grew he put Walter in the awkward position of having a brother five years his junior who was better at almost everything, even sports. In this last predicament at least Walter was not alone. At the inevitable touch football games spawned by big family gatherings even the other dads agreed the only way to deal with Charlie was just to knock him down.

Richard, like all of us, was fascinated by Charlie, but as I say especially drawn to Walter who in turn was particularly earnest and affectionate in his adoption of Richard as an uncle. One spring day at Elaine's — I think it was her annual azalea party because it was a little chilly — Richard was sitting on a bench in the backyard when Walter approached him, looking both more shy and more earnest than usual.

"Uncle Richard?"

"Yes?"

"I am having my Confirmation this year."

"Excellent! May we have the honor of attending?"

"Um. Actually I was hoping you would be my sponsor."

VII

Richard told me later he was completely shocked, overwhelmed, and flattered. No one else was even surprised.

"Walter, thank you so much. I am so honored. When do we do it and where's the church?"

"Italy! Holy Uncle is doing it!"

I don't know what Richard would have said to that if he'd had the chance to say anything. No matter, for at that moment Charlie, who had been hiding in a nearby bush leaped out and shouted in triumph, "Ha, ha! No backs, no backs, no pennytax! Now you have to come! And I'm having my First Communion."

VIII

All the Poles were fanatic bargain hunters. We were still in starving-writer mode and thrilled when Stan turned up some utterly obscure airline that ran not quite regular but amazingly cheap flights to the Eternal City. We were a little less thrilled when we arrived somewhere in the dark underbelly of JFK, in a terminal that smelled like cattle headed for the slaughterhouse. The lines in front of the ticket counters seemed miles long: babies crying, men shouting, women ululating in who knows how many languages, their luggage consisting mostly of cartons tied with twine. I half-expected goats and chickens. When we finally got on board, the first thing we noticed was the Pan Am logo on the seatbelts. Pan Am had been defunct for years. Not a good sign.

A two-hour delay on the tarmac, service bordering on rude—the other side of the border—and food bad even by airline standards. No fear. We missed most of it courtesy of Ambien and arrived Sunday morning at Rome's Leonardo da Vinci/FiumicinoAirport.

We had travelers checks, but on a Sunday I thought it would be wise to change some money at the airport *cambio* while I could. I got us about three hundred dollars, a lot of money by our standards, and plenty to cover any contingency until the banks opened Monday. Then in the interest of economy we decided to skip the taxi line and take a subway into town.

Big mistake.

There were about five of them, I'd say, and they worked with the practiced precision of a SWAT team. The first thing they did was separate us by jostling Richard to the door and me to the center of the train. Then one of them "tripped" into me and started shouting indignantly: I was a selfish American taking up too much room. Then the man who slammed into me started shouting at me too. The train was crowded and lurched a lot, so it was easy to keep me off balance and easy to keep me distracted by yelling in my face while they did it.

Finally one of them "accidentally" knocked my hat off, which made me mad enough to shout back, which caused the group of German teenagers nearby to glare at me reproachfully. I felt hands on my waist. When the train lurched into the next station I yanked myself out of their grip. Then the train stopped, the doors opened, and all five of them slipped off.

The young Germans were scowling at me. They kept scowling even after a man with a British accent called out, "Miss? Miss!" He pointed to my gaping belly pack. "You've been robbed."

Our original plan had been to spend four days in Rome sightseeing, a similar stretch in Castel Gandolfo to include the Confirmation, a few days in Florence, and back home. The manager of the little hotel near the Trevi fountain was sympathetic. He let us check in even though we had lost our credit cards and travelers checks and even let us have a small cash advance. His only request was that we file an official police report.

Margaret Thatcher once called English "the language of democracy." In certain parts of the world, however, it is the language of a big sign worn around the neck: "Wallet in back pocket. Please help yourself." At the *posto di polizia* our fellow crime victims were from all over the English-speaking world. An American couple had been robbed at their hotel. Some New Zealanders had their luggage lifted. A group of Canadian backpackers had been relieved of their packs. Two Australians had lost their wallets on the notorious Number 64 bus. Running from Rome's central train station to St. Peter's Square, the 64 is a legend among hapless travelers, always loaded with tourists, and a pickpocket's happy hunting ground.

We called the credit card companies. Visa was worthless. AmEx was super. We'd have a new card and replacement checks the next day. Still the only money in our pockets for the next twenty-four hours was the advance they'd given us at the hotel.

With the little cash we had we got something to eat

from a street cart and sat down by the Trevi fountain. We shared a Coke, pricey there but the ultimate comfort food for Americans abroad. A couple of kids tore past us, jostling Richard's elbow. A stream of the precious Coke leapt out of the can and landed on the shoulders of some Germans on the tier below us. They looked around angrily. We tiptoed away.

In the morning I felt queasy and depressed. Jet lag, I told myself, plus some post-mugging thing. But we didn't have time to mope around. We had an appointment at the Vatican Museum.

A New York friend who worked at a foundation with interests in religious art had hooked us up with a curator at the Vatican who'd offered us a private tour of his stomping grounds. As it turned out he would be on vacation when we would be in Rome, but he had delegated the task to the best kind of guide any museum can provide: a security guard who'd spent decades on the floor, hearing dozens of different tour guides and contemplating the works he guarded. Try it some time. Ask an older guard at the Met about your favorite Monet and see how much you learn; I mean besides the fact that it's actually, you know, Manet.

Short, dark, and blunt, our guy told us solemnly, "The *Musei Vaticani* is a big place, a collection of museums. There are paintings; there are artifacts; we even have a few rocks some Americans brought back from the moon. So it is best to decide beforehand what you would most like to concentrate on."

Immediately Richard replied, "I would like to see the Raphael *Stanze*."

Our guide nodded approvingly. "Then we will leave the moon rocks for those who like that sort of thing. This way, please."

In 1503 Giuliano della Rovere was elected Pope Julius II. His predecessor, Pius III, had reigned for scarcely a month; Pius had succeeded Alexander VI, scion of the infamous Borgia clan and della Rovere's longtime rival. Upon his succession Julius set about cleaning house. He refused to live in the Borgia apartments, which he said reeked of Alexander, and had the rooms directly below it decorated as his private residence. In 1508 he commissioned Raphael to paint the four rooms that make up the *Stanze*.

The School of Athens is the most famous fresco in the *Stanze*. It depicts a gathering of the giants of philosophy debating the nature of Truth. At center stage are Aristotle clutching a copy of the Ethics and holding out a flat tempering hand with palm turned toward the Earth and Plato holding a copy of Timaeus under his arm and pointing heavenward. On the staircase below them sprawls Diogenes, half-naked and rather pointedly ignoring them. Fifty-five other figures complete the scene. Socrates works hard to keep the attention of a bored young man; Euclid sketches triangles on a chalkboard. A brooding Heraclitus sits with his head down, pen in hand, but clearly not making anything like Euclid's progress.

The real fun is picking out the caricatures. Plato with his flowing beard and stern features is actually a portrait of Leonardo da Vinci; the triangulating Euclid is Bramante, architect of St. Peter's and one of Raphael's mentors. Peeking out over Ptolemy's shoulder on the right is Raphael himself, beardless but with a certain world-weariness in his eyes. He would be dead before finishing the fourth *stanze*.

The hands-down favorite is Heraclitus. Chin propped on one fist, twiddling a pen between his fingers, the hulking, sulking, scowling figure caricatures not only Michelangelo but also his style. It was almost certainly added after Raphael had managed to steal a forbidden peak at the Sistine ceiling, also commissioned by Julius, on which the older artist had been at work for years.

"Raphael died quite young," our guide was saying. "Thirty-seven, I believe. Some say he died of Roman fever, others say overwork. He was working on these rooms when he died. So perhaps he died for these frescoes."

I squinted at Heraclitus. He didn't look well either. And as I was just beginning to realize, I wasn't feeling so great myself. I interrupted our guide to say I was just going to find a bathroom.

VIII

The next thing I remember I was lying face up on one of the most glorious marbled floors in Italy, looking up at a frescoed ceiling, wondering how I'd gotten there.

Blank for the next few minutes. Then a wheelchair and I am being bundled into it. How nice. But for some reason we don't go anywhere. Instead I am surrounded by Italians arguing. Arguing over me, apparently. I speak a little Italian but that hardly matters. Even to a half-conscious American the pantomime is clear enough. They are arguing, so help me, over who is to have the honor of pushing the wheelchair. Blank again. Then we are moving. In procession, but in a curious start-and-stop manner. In an eminently just resolution of the wheelchair dispute, the man who had lost the honor of propelling me through the museum had been given, as a sort of consolation prize, the job of leading our little parade a few steps at a time, at each stop grandly calling out, "Attenzione! Attenzione!" Not surprisingly he got exactly that, the full attention of art lovers from around the world who would otherwise have been blissfully ignorant of our little drama. At each stop, having grandly achieved the crowd's "attenzione" he would, with gestures positively operatic, disperse the onlookers he had so artfully gathered in the first place. To my dying day I will believe he was one of the spear-carriers from that damned *Aïda* at the Baths. No, a torchbearer. He would have insisted on a torch.

Back at our hotel I settled into a pattern of staggering to the bathroom, staggering back, then lying in bed sweating and shaking until it was time to stagger again. Richard called Kasia ("She's the only doctor we know in this country") who, after amusing herself by complimenting me on choosing to faint in front of the *second* most famous work of art in the museum ("if you'd fainted under the Sistine ceiling you might not have been found for days"), declared that she would not only catch the next train into the city but would deploy her formidable and well-connected mother as well.

A few minutes later the phone rings. Richard picks up.

"Hello—uh, *pronto*? Yes. Yes, here she is." He handed me the phone. "It's some friend of Kasia's mother."

"Hello," I croaked.

"Signora Vigilante?" a high, hesitant Italian voice said. "Good afternoon. I understand you are seeeck?"

"Yeesss," I moaned. "I am sooo sick." I proceeded to pour out my symptoms in graphic detail.

There was a pause.

"I am Cardinal Angelini," the voice said at last. "I will send my personal physician to you right away. Try to rest. Of course I pray for your recovery also. Goodbye."

Richard took the phone back. "What's wrong?"

"Nothing." I closed my eyes. "I just hope I'm hallucinating."

VIII

When Kasia showed up an hour or so later she took one look at me and burst out laughing. "Susan. How wonderful to see you. But you look like shit."

"Thanks," I muttered. "Do you know a Cardinal Angelini?"

"Of course. He is head of the Vatican commission on health care."

"Arrrghhhh."

Richard opened a bottle of wine, and he and Kasia shared a glass while I faded in and out of consciousness. The cardinal's physician arrived. He turned out to be professor of surgery at the medical school as well as a partner at an exclusive private clinic. He explained, with Kasia interpreting his uncertain English, that I was dehydrated and with my history (I had been in the hospital with peritonitis two summers before, when I saw Sharon in her postulant garb) I should check into his clinic for a few days. The clinic was ferociously expensive and not covered by our insurance, but Richard's doctor brother Kevin had warned us away from Italian public hospitals.

Richard asked the obvious question. "Does your clinic take American Express?"

Don't leave home without it.

I staggered into the Casa di Cura at about five in the afternoon. The tanned, elegant young woman at the reception desk looked me up and down and decided she was done for the day. We were too late, she told us disdainfully. Come back tomorrow.

"Ma . . . ma . . ." I searched frantically for words. "But the *professore* said I could check in now," I said.

She made a show of shuffling papers together and clearing her desk. "Impossibile," she said briskly. Reception is "chiuso." Closed. She stretched out a manicured hand and started to slide her window shut.

I'd had a couple of long days. I'd been robbed, I'd been poisoned, I had given up my hotel room, and I was sick as a dog.

I grabbed the edge of the receptionist's window. She opened her large, lovely, mascaraed eyes wide and uttered a shocked, "Signora!"

That did it. I slammed the window open. "Listen, sweetheart," I snarled. "I'm not going anywhere. I am checking into this hospital, tonight. And you're not going anywhere until you've admitted me. Now. Understand? NOW!"

A little New York goes a long way. She clammed up and started filling out forms.

The rare elation that comes from defeating an Italian bureaucrat wafted me into my room.

And what a room. I'd been in a few hospitals in my day, and I'd never seen anything like this. White linen towels, down pillows, gleaming marble floors. French doors, leading on to a private balcony, a garden, with a fountain, of course, below. It was more beautiful than any hotel I'd ever even seen, let alone stayed in.

As I settled back against the pillow a waiter in a

spotless white jacket brought iced tea on a silver tray. Another waiter suggested a cocktail. (There were several bars in the hospital.) Dinner arrived shortly afterward: poached sole with a white wine sauce and a lovely pear tart.

Richard had a bright idea: "Let's not bother with hotels any more. Next time let's just beef up our medical insurance and come straight here."

Two days later *il professore* agreed to discharge me, provided I promised never to eat from a street cart again. He also urged me to eat a lot of *amb*. "Ham," whispered one of his students. "For the salt."

I was in no shape to get on a train, so someone at the hospital called us a cab.

It was early afternoon when we finally got to Castel Gandolfo. The taxi squeezed itself down a few narrow streets and came to a halt at the edge of the town square.

Richard looked out the window. "I don't believe it."

At one of the cafés, seated at a table with Kasia and the boys, were four nuns. One of them gave me a big smile.

I went tearing out of the cab.

IX

It turns out the Sister Evangelists had all sorts of paperwork and procedures to go through in Rome along the way to getting their order officially recognized. At least two would have had to come to the city, and there were only four professed sisters, and Sharon's father was paying, so why not come for the Confirmation/First Communion and a chance to meet Holy Father? We met the sisters, a lanky blonde with a broad Southern drawl, who had taken the name Sister John Paul, and a dark, short one, whose name escapes me now. Then there was Mother Superior, the foundress, a former Dominican who suffered from diabetes, walked with a cane, and combined a first-rate mind and a commanding presence with motherly warmth, generosity, and a powerful intuition. Special, and one knew it immediately.

The boys naturally were thrilled to hear we had been robbed and made us repeat every detail; Charlie sure he would have "defeated them" had he been with us. All too soon it was time for the Zajacs to go in for the evening, the nuns as well. (Even traveling they would rise at five thirty for morning prayer.) The Zajacs would have little time to see us the next day, Sunday, preparing for the ceremony the day after. But Kasia offered to arrange for us to come to Holy Father's Sunday morning mass in the courtyard. "You would have to get up rather early . . ."

"Then she may not come."

A short, gray-haired woman in a tailored navy dress stood beside the table, her hands clasped behind her back. *La Dottoressa.* Kasia's mother, Rasia. Everyone except me stood up.

"Susan, Richard," Kasia said, "this is my mother."

I started to get up, but one look from Kasia's mother made me stay where I was. "It's nice to see you," I said feebly. "Thank you so much for your help. I . . ."

"It was no trouble. I am sorry you were ill, but you are recovering; that is what matters." She studied me with professional detachment. "You are very pale. You need rest. We will not look for you at mass in the morning. You will sleep. Now I will give you a kiss." She took my face in her hands and planted a firm, no-nonsense kiss on my cheek. She looked at Richard. "Take her home."

In the movie *His Girl Friday* Rosalind Russell introduces the sweet but dull man she is about to marry to her ex-husband Cary Grant. The fiancé, impressed by Grant's suave manners and quick wit, tells Russell, "I like him, Hildy. I think he's very charming."

"He comes by it naturally," Russell shoots back. "His grandfather was a snake."

I'm with Roz. Nothing gets my guard up like charm.

They say Ted Bundy oozed the stuff.

Just as there are a lot of charmers you can't trust, all too often the really good people in one's life are completely devoid of social appeal. I mean the rocks, the ones you know you can turn to in a crisis with complete confidence that they will behave like heroes, but who are just awful at dinner or cocktails or anywhere else being a hero is not what's called for just at the moment. People who are good without being nice, just as plenty of nice people are no damn good.

Thank God for heroes. But they can be hard to be around.

As a schoolgirl in Cracow, Rasia was a Girl Guide. She loved the outdoor life, camping and hiking in the summertime, skiing and skating in the winter. And like every Pole I have ever met, she loved Poland.

When the Nazis overran the country in 1939 Rasia and most of her Girl Guide friends did what they could to fight back, mostly acting as couriers for the hopelessly outmatched Polish resistance. Like many of her friends Rasia was caught. She was nineteen years old.

She was thrown into prison in Cracow. All day, from dawn until long after dark, she listened to gunshots in the prison yard as one after another of the prisoners, including most of her young friends, were executed. Once as she was being dragged to yet another interrogation session she met a friend from the Girl Guides in the corridor. "Tell them it was me," the girl whispered.

"Whatever they ask, blame everything on me." Moments later Rasia heard the shots from the yard.

For some six months Rasia and her friends were held in Cracow. They passed the time between interrogations praying for the souls of their murdered friends and savaged homeland. Then one day the girls got word that things were about to change.

Years later Rasia would recall that when the girls first heard they were to be taken from the prison and relocated to a "camp," they were actually encouraged. Camping in the open air—what else did a Girl Guide live for? Finally they were going to get away from this awful place, away from the continual explosions of gunfire and the smell of death, and to the good fresh countryside.

They had been more than two years in Ravensbrück when, one day, along with a handful of other Polish prisoners, Rasia was summoned to the infirmary. An attendant ordered them to undress, and they were plunged into a warm bath. After three years of alternating filth and ice-water washes the bath should have been the most welcome of luxuries. But, difficult as it must have been to awake a new kind of dread in these women after years of unimaginable brutality, they found something in the attendants' manner terrifying.

Soon Rasia was separated from the others and found herself in what looked like a hospital operating room. For hours Rasia lay on a table while men and women in white coats poked and prodded her, at first speaking freely among themselves but then clamming up when they realized she understood German. The last thing she remembered was an orderly taking a brush of mercurochrome and painting lines on her leg, as if drawing a map . . .

As the Nazis retreated they murdered most of the surviving victims of the medical experimentation units, but by some combination of guile and grace Rasia survived. She became a doctor, a psychiatrist who specialized in treating survivors of the camps, and later one of Karol Wojtyla's brain trust in Poland, working on pro-life and family issues. Her whole life was given to the service of others and through them to serving Christ. But she bore always the marks of her youth and she was a ferociously difficult woman. Kasia once told me that her mother was a wonderful human being who unfortunately could not take seriously any human suffering that would not impress a concentration camp victim. She frightened her children, her husband, and for all I know the Holy Father. She certainly frightened me. But it seemed I would be safe. I was her patient now and under her protection.

Sunday morning we were sitting in the little breakfast room of the Bucci, me practicing eating my *amb* European style (fork left, knife right) when a brown and white blur whipped into the room.

"I'm sorry, I'm sorry, I'm sorry I'm late," Sharon

arrived, flushed and breathless. She grabbed a chair. "Oh good, coffee. Thank you, Jesus,"

"Where are the others?" Richard asked.

"They had to go in to Rome." She knocked back a *caffe latte* and signaled for another cup. "OK, I'm starting to feel human again. Sue—stand up a second—what are you wearing? Huh. It's—cute. I'm not sure about the color though. But you're still pretty pale. So, what shall we do today?"

Before I could reply she was off and running. "We absolutely have to do some shopping. I love my life, Sue, but I can't tell you how much I miss shopping. You can get some great deals in this town. Especially scarves. And handbags. Mother should be back sometime after siesta, so I have to be back here by then." She drained the last of her cup. "So. Are we ready?"

"If you don't mind I think I'll skip the scarf hunt," Richard said.

"That's fine. We'll see you later." Sharon stood up. "Come on, Sue. Let's hit the stores!"

We walked through the narrow streets to the piazza. "You know what's great about Italy? Lots of nuns. People don't stare at me the way they do in the States." She waved to a little girl who was smiling at her from across the road. "I still don't like that part of it. New York is bad enough, but oh, my goodness, Sue, Mississippi. It's like you're from Mars."

"Don't say you weren't warned."

She laughed. "I would never say that." We stopped in front of a window. "Let's go inside. I've always liked this place."

Even without customers the tiny shop felt cramped. Racks of scarves and blouses, belts, bags, and leather purses crowded the floor. Every inch of wall space was lined with shelves, every shelf was overloaded with pictures of the pope, statues, all the usual Italian tchotchka shop stuff.

She held up a scarf and peeked at herself in a mirror. "Ugh, brown."

"Your habit's brown."

"In the first place, that wasn't my idea; it was the Lord's. And in the second place, at least it's a Dior."

"It's a knockoff."

"Shh!"

After the Second Vatican Council, women's religious orders in the United States "modernized" their habit. Nuns' attire went through many permutations in those heady years: first shorter veils, then shorter skirts, then just about anything until the few orders that kept any kind of habit at all ended up looking like lady golfers on a bad day. One American order, however, did one smart thing; they called in Christian Dior.

Dior came up with three easy pieces: a full-sleeved, ankle-skimming shift in white; a contrasting "scapular" (a shoulder-width apron that hangs over the shift front and back); and a short, elbow-length cape, plus whatever style veil the order chose. Women of all shapes looked so good in it that new orders throughout the land had been copying it ever since.

Sharon returned the scarf to the rack. Then she pulled down half a dozen more and held them up in front of me. "No. No, not quite. We'll just have to keep shopping." She took another look in the mirror, gave her veil a discreet adjustment, and sighed. "Honestly, Sue, it's the cape that saves this outfit. Let's go downstairs."

The basement of the shop was like a cave with halogen lights shining from the low-beamed ceiling and gravel crunching underfoot. The shelves that lined the rough stone walls were crammed with every variety of Italian ceramic: colorful pitchers, platters, candlesticks. Here also were much nicer versions of the cheap statuary upstairs. There were Nativity sets, holy water fonts . . . Sharon picked up a small terracotta statue, about six inches high, of a bearded man in a black robe. He had thin gray hair and intense beady black eyes. One hand was held up in the traditional gesture of blessing, a small red spot in the center of the palm.

The statue was of Padre Pio, a Franciscan monk and reputed saint, who had died in 1968. When he was still a young man he manifested the stigmata, the wounds inflicted on Christ during His crucifixion. The case for his canonization was being heard in Rome.

I looked at the statue dubiously. "Isn't this kind of . . . cheating?"

"What do you mean?"

"Well he's not a saint yet, right? What are they going to do with all these statues if they decide he isn't one? Mark them down?"

"I don't think anybody's too worried about that. He'll be canonized. Do you believe in the stigmata, Sue?"

I had to smile. This was one of the things I loved best about Sharon, the way she could ask the most profound spiritual question as if she were talking about this fall's Ralph Laurens.

"Seriously." She checked the price tag. "Do you believe in them?"

"I guess so. As far as I know no one could ever explain them in any natural sense. Not Pio's, anyway."

"But you're hedging your bets." She replaced the statue in its place on the shelf. "That's the thing about entering the convent, Sue. There's no room for hedging anymore. You jump in with both feet, or you don't jump. The longer I'm a nun the more I realize that's the choice everybody has to make."

She folded her arms. "Man, this place is damp. Are you cold?"

"It's getting to me."

"Me, too. Let's go find Kasia."

Outside the day was hot and the boys were dying to go down to the lake. Stan couldn't come—he had reading duty that morning—but Kasia agreed. We all piled into one car and drove down the hill to the crater.

It took a while but the boys finally managed to sell Sharon on going paddle boating in full nun regalia. With Richard and the boys in one boat and Sharon, Kasia, and me in another, we agreed to race to the water tower.

"It's a pity the other sisters aren't around," Kasia mused. "You and Mother paddling, Susan and I in bikinis sipping Bellinis. That would be the right way to do this." She pedaled after her sons, already far ahead of us.

"Oh yeah, great." The beads of Sharon's rosary clicked noisily as she pedaled for all she was worth.

Finally we were gaining on them. Then at a signal from Richard the boys suddenly stood up, brandished the water rifles they had hidden on board, and opened fire.

"Hey!" A stream of water caught me square in the face. "Cut it out!"

"All right! That does it!" Sharon picked up an oar and started sending tidal waves of lake water into the boys' boat. They stepped up the assault. Kasia and I kept pedaling. We passed them.

"Come back here, you cowards!" Charlie yelled. "Come back and fight!"

"Eat my dust! Mist! Whatever!"

A long siesta back at the Bucci. Another amazing simple dinner at the restaurant out back, overlooking the lake. On the way back up to the piazza we pass through the living room of the Bucci where the men of the family are sprawled on the overstuffed sofa transfixed by something on the TV. It's Tina Turner, all shimmering spangles and shimmying thighs belting out a ballad. The father of the house, catching our eyes, gestures toward Tina with two expansive hands and utters a single word: *immortale.*

Kasia looked amused. "I think your husband is in heaven,"

Richard had found a couple of philosophy professors to argue with. By the looks of things they were having a blast. I thought I recognized one of them, a priest in his fifties with wavy brown hair and a big friendly smile. "Do I know that guy?"

She nodded. "You've probably seen pictures of him, back in our apartment. He's an old friend of the Holy Father's. Very nice man."

Stan came wandering across the piazza and sat down heavily. "Walter is asleep. Charlie will be bouncing around until daybreak, I'm afraid."

"If he sleeps at all I'll be happy," Kasia said. "He is so excited about tomorrow"

"Well, it's a big day," I said.

Stan grinned at me. "So you are too excited to sleep too?"

"No. No, no."

"Such a lie."

A burst of laughter came from the philosophers' table. "Somebody must've scored," Kasia remarked. "Does anyone know what they're arguing about?"

"Oh, just chitchat. The true nature of freedom. The relationship between conscience and power. Whether the dignity of man resides in his status as a loving subject, or his ability to attain objective knowledge of creation."

"Oh, the usual."

We left the doors to the balcony open, partly to catch the breeze off the lake and partly because I figured if the alarm didn't wake us the rising sun would. Richard tested the clock about ten times, anyway, then finally drifted off. I lay there, staring at the ceiling. Finally I gave up and slipped out onto the balcony.

The lake was silent. The crew teams had gone home, and there were no lights along the shoreline for after-hours bathers. To my left the dome of the Vatican Observatory stood watch over the sky. The *Specola Vaticana* was a relative newcomer to town. Established in the 1930s, it replaced an older observatory near St. Peter's. Astronomers work nights. I wasn't the only one contemplating the heavens tonight.

Was I nervous about meeting him? Please! Of course not!

Besides, I'd already met him once.

When John Paul II came to America in 1979, one

of his stops was St. Patrick's Cathedral in New York. I was standing with the crowds outside. New Yorkers can greet the most amazing spectacle with a yawn, but the pope was taking the city by storm. People were packed shoulder to shoulder for blocks, hoping to catch a glimpse. When he suddenly appeared on the Fifth Avenue steps, the crowd went wild. I'm five feet one inch tall, so you can imagine how much I could see. Then suddenly a blond man standing next to me who spoke no English smiled, picked me up, and hoisted me onto his shoulders. Above the heads of the crowd I waved and yelled, "Holy Father! Holy Father! Welcome to America! Viva il papa!"

And I swear, he saw me. And he smiled at me and waved back, exactly the way I was waving at him.

Of course everyone in the crowd felt like that. It was one of his gifts. It was in fact one of his most fundamental beliefs: that every single solitary human being matters because he has inestimable value in the eyes of God.

I stood up and took one last look at the night sky.

Stars, *stelle*; one of my few Italian words. I learned it from Dante. *Inferno, Purgatorio,* and *Paradiso* all end with "stars": "L'amor che move il sole e l'altre stelle." ["The love that moves the sun and the other stars."]

The Greeks looked at the night sky and saw a hunter and his dogs, fighting a bull. I had never managed to locate Taurus. Just the hunter, Orion, and that was only because it held some of the brightest stars in the sky, and the row of stars that made up the hunter's belt was pretty obvious.

Of course there was no big hunter in the sky, no dogs or bulls. Thousands of years ago someone drew imaginary lines between the points of light and came up with the idea of Orion. The hunter was an invention, a story. The connections were imaginary.

But the stars were real. And not one of them was an accident.

Everything happens for a reason, I thought. Even if you never know what the reason is.

X

The streets were still empty. The storefronts were closed, the stuccoed houses still shuttered, the red geraniums in the window boxes still nodding under the weight of the morning dew. The pavement was still wet too. My high heels kept getting stuck in the ridges as I slipped over the cobblestones, leaving me bowlegged as I flailed about, trying to keep my balance.

Richard was half a block ahead of me. "Hurry!" he tossed over his shoulder. "We're going to be late!" Let him wear the heels next time, I thought.

The piazza was deserted. We hurried past the fountain and the empty cafés and up the cobblestone incline to the palace gate. We knocked on the heavy wooden door, panting.

Immediately a young Swiss Guard appeared. He gave us a subdued salute and handed us over to two men in black suits waiting just inside the gate. They led us across the interior courtyard to a side door and let us into the palace. Once we were inside the guys in the suits disappeared, and we were left in the hands of a tiny Vietnamese monsignor.

All smiles and bows the monsignor said something

that no doubt sounded to him like "buon giorno," and we said something that sounded like "buon giorno," to us.

The monsignor held out his hand in a "walk this way" gesture. "Prego!"

"Grazie!" we said.

Then he took off. *Fast*.

As he scurried down the long hallways, we were dimly aware that the floors were absolutely breathtaking, with intricate designs of a dozen different types of marble — golden yellows, chalky whites, muted shades of red and green. Above all it was blindingly polished marble, and as we learned within a couple seconds, extremely slippery. Now Richard in his leather soles was having just as much difficulty as I.

Our choices seemed few and all bad: race after the little Vietnamese and fall on our rear ends in the papal palace, or lag behind and become lost in the labyrinth, miss our chance to meet the pope, and disappoint our young friend waiting for us to do our sacramental duty only to surface hours later as accused terrorists, or, even more shameful, journalists.

The little monsignor made a compromise of sorts. He would race to the end of a hallway. At each corner he would pause and look back at us beseechingly. We would race after him as fast as we dared until we had just caught up. Then he would smile, stretch out his hand, and bow and say, "prego," pointing for us to go ahead. We would reply, "grazie," imagining we must be near our destination, and walk on in a more dignified manner. Then he would start running again, leaving us far behind.

Corner.

Stop.

"Prego."

Point.

"Grazie."

Walk in dignified manner.

Fall behind.

Run.

Corner.

Stop.

"Prego."

Point.

"Grazie." Walk in dignified manner. Run. This was repeated so many times in that seventeenth-century palace that we began to get a little punch drunk, the way you feel when you've been making left turns around a parking lot too long looking for an empty space. By now the walking bit had dropped out entirely and it was more like: Run fast (little monsignor). Run slow (Vigilantes). Stop and wait (little monsignor again). Slow and nod while passing by (us). "Prego." Point. "Grazie." (Us, on the fly.) And run. Which is how, after chasing the monsignor down I don't know how many hallways and seeing the little priest do the prego-point one last time, we turned yet another corner, careened into the tiny chapel, and skidded to a halt just short of tripping over the Vicar of Christ on Earth, on his knees, deep in prayer.

After the muted marbles of the corridors, the pope's private chapel is something of a shock. Gaudy twentieth-century murals cover the walls, bright reds and crayon-box blues splash across a glaring white background. A stark modern altar takes center stage at the front.

But none of this registered until later. At first all I could see were those shoulders.

John Paul II was bigger than I thought he would be. He knelt in the center of the aisle, with his shoulders hunched up and his forehead resting on his clasped hands. The white worsted wool of his cassock strained across his back, as if a hundred Italian tailors couldn't keep up with this one Polish pope. He knelt without moving. He had been there for hours.

I looked at that back, those shoulders, those hands. All I could think was "mountain."

A mountain, a place of refuge. "Flee to the mountains," a safe but wild place, protecting but challenging, your last, best hope, but not an easy one. "I have been to the mountaintop." I have seen the truth. Mountain air, the purest on earth, the timeless healer of stricken lungs and broken hearts. The place where all becomes clear at last.

I looked at John Paul II and I thought, "This man is a mountain."

Someone touched Richard's elbow and showed us to our seats. We slipped into a pew.

On the opposite side of the chapel was Kasia, in a flowered silk dress I recognized as one of Sharon's pre-convent favorites. Two seats away from Kasia was her mother, looking forbidding in tailored navy blue linen. I knew that dress too: Kasia found it on one of her thrift shop runs.

Wedged between Kasia and *La Dottoressa* were the two boys: Walter, looking schoolboy smart in a blazer and flannel trousers that Richard and he had bought together for the occasion; Charlie looking every inch his dashing little self in a white bomber jacket and black slacks. Both boys wore white roses pinned to their lapels. In the row behind them Stan and Kasia's father knelt with their hands loosely clasped. Stan looked thoughtfully toward the altar. His father-in-law seemed to be looking at something that wasn't there. A little smile played at his lips.

On our side of the aisle the first two rows were taken up by Sharon and the nuns. They knelt with their heads bowed and their hands folded, their carefully ironed veils hanging in sharp, identical folds down their backs, like flags on a windless day.

The Holy Father prayed for some time. Perhaps twenty minutes. Then he stood up. For a moment his forehead creased sharply. Kasia had told me his hip was giving him a lot of trouble that summer. His forehead smoothed again as if he were putting the pain aside. He looked as if he were still in the middle of a conversation. He looked uninterrupted.

And then mass began. There was no "good morning" or "we are gathered here today to celebrate" as there would have been in any American church: no greeting, no announcement, nothing so jarring. We just slipped into the mass as if we were all being drawn into that same uninterrupted conversation.

Like every other pope watcher, I had read accounts of papal masses that went something like, "John Paul II is a powerful presence in the liturgy. In his hands the sacrament of the altar takes on a different meaning. . . ." My experience bore no resemblance to any of those tales. For me the most powerful impression was not of his presence but his absence. As mass began he seemed to recede. I am a contemporary American woman who's as star-struck as the next girl and certainly no stranger to distraction at mass. But that summer morning, in that tiny chapel with the most famous man in the world a few steps away, all I focused on was the Eucharist. That was John Paul's gift to us. Not presence but absence. He led us to Jesus. We followed where he went.

When the time came for the Confirmation, Richard stood up and edged out of the pew to play his part in the ceremony.

Maybe it was his black suit. Maybe no one had

thought to mention we were Americans. But for some reason both the pope and his assistants explained everything to Richard in Italian, a language of which he understands perhaps three words. Richard decided to deal with this misunderstanding by nodding and looking solemn, which had the effect of suggesting he understood every word, while desperately trying to figure out what to do next. Fortunately it was a simple ceremony.

A priest murmured something in Richard's ear. He nodded and placed his hand on Walter's shoulder. A priest stood next to the pope, holding a tray with a small gold cup and a couple of wads of cotton. The Holy Father touched his thumb in the cup, then made the sign of the cross on Walter's forehead. The priest murmured into Richard's ear again. He nodded and took his hand off the boy's shoulder. Someone wiped the oil off Walter's forehead with the cotton.

When it was time for Communion, Charlie went first. The pope placed the Eucharist on the little boy's tongue, and he bowed his head. The pope gave Communion to Walter next. Then he took each boy's face in his hands and kissed them twice, once on each cheek. He looked solemn and loving. The boys were solemn too.

The boys returned to their seats; so did the pope. Everyone else received the Host from one of the other priests.

After Communion everyone meditated for a while. Only then did it dawn on me that, for the first time that

I could remember, for the past hour all my attention had been on God. Not on my surroundings or my friends or even on the pope. For a long time afterward, all I would remember of that morning was the Eucharist and the feeling that I was really breathing for the first time.

The mass ended as quietly as it had begun.

The Holy Father left the altar by a side door. We filed out the back.

In the hallway the boys were surrounded. Grandparents, parents, and friends hugged them and congratulated them. "I can't get over Charlie." Richard shook his head. "He looked like a little saint in there. Did you see him after Communion? He looked like a painting."

"Ultimate proof of the transforming power of the Eucharist," I murmured. "I thought Kasia was going to cry."

Richard nodded. "Well, her boys are growing up."

I looked over at the boys. Walter had his brother in a headlock. "That'll be the day."

Kasia came over and gave me a hug. "So," she whispered, "what do you think of this dress? Can you guess where I got it?"

I laughed. "It looks good on you," I said.

"Thanks." Kasia laughed back. "Holy Father remembered it, of course. Sharon wore it when Charlie was baptized here."

The Holy Father reappeared. We stood in a line to take our turns kissing his ring and being introduced. He hugged the boys and greeted Kasia and Stan warmly.

Then at the sight of Sharon and her nuns, the pontiff lit up like a Christmas tree. "And here," he boomed, "is Sharon! Oh, but no," he corrected himself, laughing, "Now I must say . . ."

"Sister Stephen Marie!" Sharon sung back, practically jumping into the man's arms. I had never seen a more radiant smile than the one she gave John Paul. He looked pretty happy too.

He kissed her on the forehead and looked at her, murmuring something. Sharon murmured something back. Then she remembered she had a duty to perform.

I saw her shake off her girlish glow and try to assume a more businesslike attitude. I had seen Sharon attempt this many times. It had never worked out very well. So I was holding my breath now, knowing she wanted to make a good impression, to show the others that she was turning into a really mature nun.

"Holy Father," Sharon said, "this is my superior, Mother Michael."

Mother Michael was leaning on her cane. As she took the pope's hand I noticed he held it up at a much higher level than he had for anyone else, so she wouldn't feel obliged to kneel as many of the faithful do when kissing his ring. They talked for a minute in low voices. Though they had never met before they seemed like old colleagues, comfortable with each other, full of mutual respect.

"And this is Sister Marie . . ."

The little dark nun practically jumped up and down as she took the pope's hand. Sharon moved on quickly to Sister John Paul.

"and this is . . . this is . . ."

A look of horror came over Sharon's face. I had seen this look before too. Oh, my God, I thought. She's spacing on the name.

"John Paul!" Sharon burst out. "This is John Paul!"

The pope's eyes darted from the other nun's face to Sharon. The pope looked at her carefully and lowered his voice. "Sharon," he stage whispered, tapping his breast, "I'm John Paul."

For a second Sharon looked blank. Then all of a sudden she seemed to get a grip on things. "I mean, this is *Sister* John Paul. That's her name too."

The pope gave everyone a rosary from a little silver tray the Vietnamese priest held for him. When he got to Richard, Kasia introduced him as a dear friend from New York. Every time we met the Holy Father after that he would say to my husband, "Ah, New York! Good to see you again!"

I watched the introductions carefully because I was hoping to pick up a few pointers on the thing I felt most nervous about: the ring kiss.

All bishops wear a ring as a sign of their office. It is

the practice among Roman Catholics, when meeting a bishop, to kiss this ring. Not all bishops go along with the custom. I have met a few (American) bishops who were rather firmly against it (you could tell by the way they twisted their hands into a regular handshake at the first sign of you trying anything else). But it is ancient custom, and one that is respected in the Vatican.

Kissing a man's ring not being the sort of thing I did every day, I was a little nervous about it. What if I missed? Or slobbered? Was I supposed to just touch my lips to the ring or give it a real smack?

And then what was the correct posture for kissing the pope's ring? Was I supposed to go down on one knee, as I was told way back in second grade? Or was I just supposed to bow?

The group was not being much help. When the pope greeted the Zajacs, Stan went down on one knee, but Kasia bowed. Richard took the pope's hand, lifting it slightly, bowed from the waist, and touched lips to the ring. I was impressed by how dignified Richard looked, not at all awkward or shy, but like he did this every day.

Then it was my turn. I had been horrified by the thought of this moment for weeks. Does that seem absurd? There are people to whom it must, the sort of people who say, "Oh, I'm so shy" in the midst of breaking into conversation with perfect strangers or flirting their way across a room. But I really am shy. It's a dominant force in my life. Richard once gave me that Myers-Briggs personality test that companies use to figure out whether you are suited for a certain job. On the Introvert/Extrovert scale I scored a perfect ten for Introvert. At college, right before I graduated, the career placement people gave me a sort of touchy-feely aptitude test that started with a lot of no-brainer questions like "do you enjoy the company of others?" and "are you a people person?" to which everybody is supposed to just answer "yes" before getting on to the real questions. Instead I told the truth. After interpreting my scores they told me they had determined my dream job: farmer. That way it could be just me and the produce.

Shyness is a big part of my spiritual life as well. I do not do the "sign of peace" at mass. While everyone around me is shaking hands I scare them all off by blowing my nose. I do not hold hands in prayer, as some people insist, especially at the dinner table. I shudder at public displays of piety. Once we knew someone who would insist on saying grace before meals—in public restaurants. The first time I let it go by. The second time I accidentally spilled a water glass into her lap. She's never done it again. I do not have any use for Christians I barely know smiling that bland, grinning-idiot-Christian smile at me, and telling me what "the Lord" told them to do that day. It's enough to make you start cheering for the lions.

He made it OK.

It was my first experience of John Paul II's incredible

tact, not to mention his ability to read people's emotions. He held out his hand as if for an ordinary American-style handshake. But just as I touched his hand he turned it very, very slightly—so slightly that if you didn't know about the ring-kissing custom, you probably would not have noticed anything out of the ordinary. What he was doing, I realized, was very subtly offering me the option. The way he'd turned his hand the ring was just about facing upward, in a position to be kissed if you were up to it, in a position to be ignored without the slightest awkwardness if you weren't.

I bowed and touched my lips to the smooth gold surface.

It made the rest of it easier, really. I mean you've just kissed the man's ring, how shy-making can the rest be?

La Dottoressa spoke up. "We will have a picture!" she announced. "With the whole family! Everyone, come over here." She started pushing and plucking at everyone, arranging us in rows. "You, stand here. Holy Father, you're here. Sisters, over here. Charlie, here; Walter, here. You and you, here."

The Holy Father caught Richard's eye and gave him an apologetic little shrug. "She is strict," he said, but he went where he was told. So did everyone else.

I am looking at the photo on my wall as I write. Everyone is laughing.

The pope left us for a moment and we followed an

attendant into the dining room. In a moment the Holy
Father reappeared smiling and lifting his hands. On his
feet were a pair of old worn slippers. "Buon giorno," he
boomed, "e buon appetito!"

Everyone laughed. Grace was said. We all sat
down.

Stan went over to the sideboard. He picked up a
platter and started going around the table with it. When
it got to me I saw the platter was laden with slices of
sausage and cheese. The meat was studded with bits of
fat the size of pennies.

"I forgot to tell you. We are having Polish breakfast this morning." Kasia spoke in a stage whisper, "You
mustn't touch it. It will send you straight back to the
hospital." Kasia signaled to a nun and said something
in Polish. "I have ordered you some toast. You can eat
that." Stan moved on with the plate.

The room hummed with conversation as people
tucked into their breakfast.

He turned to the boys and asked them if their excite-
ment over the morning had subsided yet. The boys
grinned and shook their heads. "It's all exciting," Walter
said. "Just having everyone here like this. It's just like
home. Only better."

At that first breakfast the Holy Father did everything
he could to put us at our ease and include us in the conversation. It was tough work and eventually too much

for him. I'm always quiet. Richard almost never. But at breakfast he was, as he later described it, catatonic.

Fortunately we had the nuns, all of whom seemed unabashed if respectful, something like senior girls at a private school having tea with a favorite teacher. He asked how their brand new order was going. "Wonderful, Holy Father," bubbled the dark-haired Italian-looking one. "It's growing like crazy. We have five novices."

"What! Five thousand novices, already! Magnificent." Big broad papal smile, as if to say, "I got you."

Many giggles in reply. But the dark one was undeterred. "Yes, Holy Father. In fact we think it must be a great time of grace and a great work of the Holy Spirit that there are so many new vocations in America."

The Holy Father paused thoughtfully and looked over the nuns in their newly designed and approved habits. He nodded gravely. "Yes. Yes. It must be the work of the Holy Spirit, if it has gotten Sharon to wear brown."

XI

Kasia swirled the sherry in her glass. "Stan is talking about finishing his dissertation this spring."

"That's good, isn't it?"

"If he finishes the dissertation, he will graduate. And once he graduates, his student visa will no longer be valid."

"Oh, no."

"There is the green card lottery, of course. But we have tried that before, and . . ." Kasia's voice caught in her throat. "I am so worried, Susan. If we have to go back to Poland . . . there's no future for the children there . . ." She covered her mouth with her hand.

"Can't he stall for a while? Lots of people take forever to finish their dissertations."

Kasia shook her head. "He thinks he might have a chance at a job in a college down South next fall. But he can't apply for it unless he has his PhD completed. So he's determined to finish." She blinked. "He's already nearly done, actually."

"Oh, God, Kasia." I stared into Elaine's fireplace, hoping for inspiration. None came. "There must be something you can do."

"Only pray for a green card." She rubbed her face with her hand. "And so far my prayers have not been answered."

Kasia stood up. "I'm going to see if Elaine needs any help in the kitchen."

"She's setting up dessert," Meghan said. "Susan brought brownies."

"Oh, dear. The boys have probably finished them already."

"Elaine hid them."

"You underestimate my boys." Kasia disappeared.

In the kitchen the guys were huddling together at the counter. "Uh-oh," said Richard. "Act casual, boys."

"Oh, Susan!" Stan swallowed quickly. "Wonderful brownies!"

"Yes, thank you, Aunt Susan," said Walter.

"It's rude to talk with your mouth full." Charlie smirked.

"Oh, like you never do."

"Mmph-ph-ph-ph."

"All right, boys." Elaine clapped her hands. "Take the brownies out to the dining room. I'll get the tea. We'll all sit at the table and have our dessert like civilized human beings."

"I love civilization," Kasia sighed.

Six months later they were gone. Banished to Bulgaria—where Stan would teach at the American University—because instead of dropping out of sight and becoming a cab driver, Stan did everything he was supposed to do, stayed absolutely legal, got his PhD, tried for years to get a green card legitimately. For this, he and his family were unceremoniously booted out of the country.

Now to Sharon's letters from exile were added Kasia's:

Dear Susan,

Thank you for your letters. The postal system here is not very reliable and it can take them weeks to get here. Thank you for not giving up even though you haven't heard from me!

We are living in an apartment not far from the university. The town is quite nice, especially the center which is very old. There are many cafés and stores—not much in them, but at least they make an effort.

Even so, this country is very difficult to live in. Everything you touch is badly made. We only have running water from midnight to six AM, and there is no central heating. We have four electrical heaters, one for each room, but the electricity keeps breaking down. We have had quite a few freezing nights.

There is plenty of food but most of it is not fresh, except vegetables in the summer. I wanted to make the boys a cheesecake last week. It took days of shopping but I finally thought I had all the ingredients, and on Sunday I put it all in the oven. It smelled good, but . . . well, it turned out that what I was sure was cream cheese was actually some kind of lard. So you can imagine.

I am reading my way through the university library. Other than that there is not much to do. Do you suppose you'd ever want to visit Bulgaria?

What about Italy next summer?

Love,

Kasia

Dear Aunt Susan & Uncle Richard,

Aunt Meghan is coming to visit us next month. Why do you stay home? We had water all day yesterday but not today. My father says all the Americans at the university believe in education. So stupid. Please come and see us in Italy. I miss your brownies. It will be Halloween soon in New York but not here. I am sad.

Love,

Charlie

Dear Aunt Susan & Uncle Richard,

Thank you for the early Christmas present Aunt Meghan brought. I will use the money to buy a new video game. Are you excited about the football season? Who do you think will play in the Super Bowl?

We bought a new TV, but we are having trouble hooking up our Sega Genesis to it. Overall we hate Bulgaria.

Love,

Walter

p. s. Aunt Meghan brought us your brownies. Thank you! There are none left.

PART III
John

XII

I kept praying but I never became pregnant. Eventually we began to think about adoption and even to take some serious steps in that direction. Then one day an enemy appeared.

ℴ • ℚ

"Hello! Hello! Sorry, I can't hear you! Let me check the line!"

John tickled the baby's thigh. Emma squealed. He held her foot to his ear.

"Nope, nothing wrong with the line! Wait a minute, I'm getting a call on the other foot!"

He slapped her left foot to his ear. The baby laughed, then kicked him square on the jaw.

"Ow! I think we have a short somewhere! Let me check the system!"

He went for her belly button. She shrieked.

"Boot up!" A little boy with blond hair and his father's big smile came running into the living room. "Boot up, daddy!"

"All right, boot up! Let's see what we got!" He swept

the little girl onto his shoulders and followed the boy to the computer.

Harry sat on his father's lap. A chessboard appeared on the screen. Harry looked thoughtful, then moved a pawn. "Your turn!"

My niece, who was getting bored, wriggled down from her father's shoulders and went off in search of Dean, her twin brother. He looked skeptical. "Emma's been getting him into a lot of trouble lately," my sister explained. "The other day she took my wallet out of my purse and hid it in his crib. Emma! Uh-uh, girlfriend! Away from the Christmas tree."

Emma put her hands behind her back.

"And put the teddy back, please."

Emma scowled, but hung the miniature bear back on its branch. She took Dean's hand and led him away.

The tree was up, the lights were strung, and Mary Beth was tearing open packages of tinsel. "You know," she called to her husband, "you could give me a hand here."

"No can do 'cause I'm a Jew."

"So was Jesus." She tossed him a box. "Here. Go crazy."

"Daddy? Deanie has a baby," Harry piped up.

"Mm-hmm, Deanie is a baby." My brother-in-law stood back and scrutinized his work.

"Daddy," Harry repeated. "Deanie has a baby."

"What?" He looked. "Dean, what have you got in

your—" He stuck a finger into his son's mouth. "What's this?"

"Jesus!" Harry grinned. "It's Jesus, Daddy!"

John looked at me.

"What?" I said. "It's from the Nativity set. I gave it to you last year, remember?"

He looked at his wife. "Harry found it," she told him. "It was in with the Christmas things. I let him take it out."

"Baa!" Emma waved a terracotta sheep at us. "Baa, baa!"

"OK, guys." John pried the figurines out of the twins' hands. "Let's put these where they belong, OK?" To Mary Beth, "Where do they belong?"

"On the china cabinet. Next to the menorah."

Lee had a brother. His name was John. Richard used to visit Lee at her family's apartment in New York during college breaks, so R had known John since he was eighteen and John was sixteen. I didn't meet John till almost fifteen years later.

At sixteen John was a legend of obnoxiousness, particularly devoting himself to making Lee's male friends miserable for hanging around her. Richard did not mourn when John ran away to England, and stayed for several years. But John turned out to be something of a genius. He became an early computer jock and built his own successful software consulting firm, with clients like the New York Times and major brokerage houses. "And we were worried that he wasn't doing his homework," Lee remarked later.

My sister Mary Beth was the rebel, or rather one of the rebels, in my family. Most of her rebellions were pretty tame stuff—cigarettes, hanging out with friends until all hours, longing for a motorcycle. It was only after she finished college that her "independence" started to worry me for real.

She had a good job on Wall Street, shared a decent apartment with friends, attended all the family gatherings. The trouble was her love life.

I had never met a boyfriend of MB's who did not make my hair stand on end. A bailiff who moonlighted as a bouncer in a shabby Queens bar; an alcoholic artist who supported himself by sweeping out cages in a zoo; a housepainter who thought *The Stranger* was the greatest book ever written.

I made up my mind I had to find someone for her. A fellow rebel if she insisted, but at least a rebel who worked indoors, preferably unarmed.

For a few years Lee and I had been talking about fixing MB up with John. For years, neither party was particularly interested. Finally at a moment when both were at loose ends romantically, they agreed to a blind date.

It was decided that the five of us, MB and John, plus me, Richard, and Lee—would meet for dinner at a restaurant in Little Italy.

Two things stand out in my memory about that night. The first is how John made his entrance on the scene of MB's life: late, rushing clumsily along the crowded sidewalk with his hair a mess, his jacket flapping open, and in all likelihood his fly undone as well. It was in this state that my sister first saw him. He was so worried about being late that he never even noticed the four of us lingering on the sidewalk. Instead he tore past us and barrelled right in to the restaurant, calling frantically for the Vigilante party. Months later my sister would say that the moment she laid eyes on this short, dishevelled man with the coke-bottle glasses and the generally lost look, her heart sank with the certain knowledge that this was her date.

The second memorable thing was how John made his exit, or rather how he told us to make ours. After the restaurant we stopped at a bar where the staff performed Broadway show tunes between rounds. At one point MB excused herself to find the ladies' room. As soon as she was out of earshot John turned to us and said, "You three can leave any time."

Seconds later Richard, Lee, and I found ourselves out on the street. Our shocked silence was finally broken by Lee. "Wow," she said quietly.

"Wow."

The rest, as they say, was history. Mary Beth and John were married two years later, in a ceremony presided over by a Catholic priest and a Jewish rabbi, at the United Nations Chapel in New York.

Mary Beth was stunning in a white Scaasi gown with opalescent embroidery that changed colors whenever she moved and a long, luxurious train. At the end of the ceremony the best man produced an empty glass.

This was the one Jewish tradition John insisted on. He had been practicing for months, stomping on glass after glass until there was scarcely a drinking vessel left in the house. "You know it's a lot harder than it looks," he said. "Half the time it just skids away across the floor. You have to hit it just right."

The best man set the glass on the floor and covered it with a napkin. John picked up his foot and stomped. The glass was obliterated. The crowd broke into applause. John looked around with a dazed smile, so lost in his moment of triumph that he forgot all about his bride and marched off the altar solo. So long as I live I shall never forget the sight of my sister grabbing up her train and tearing down the aisle after her husband. "Johnny! Wait for me! Wait up!"

The reception was lavish and lovely. My sister led the way onto the dance floor with a glass of champagne in one hand and the bustled-up train of her dress in the other. My brother Gene, still alive then, led his band—and the guests—in a rendition of "Gloria" that was, well, glorious. At Richard's and my wedding he'd done "Jailhouse Rock." Funny.

The newlyweds spent the night at the Plaza. The next morning John's father gave the couple a brunch at Windows on the World on the 107th floor of the World Trade Center, North Tower. A beautiful clear morning, the city stretched out before us like a still life.

"Pinch me," I said.

Lee looked out over the city. "It feels like a dream, doesn't it?"

"Maybe it is."

"Oh, no." She looked over her shoulder at the bride and groom. "This is real, all right. And we did it, Susan."

XIII

Harry was born almost a year to the day after the wedding—the twins, Dean and Emma, two years later. John moved his family from his beloved Manhattan to the absolute nearest suburb, Bronxville, right over the city line. Still childless, still ions, we were deeply caught up in the life of their little family, or at least it seemed that way to us. I am sure it did not seem that way to either my sister or to John. Families form and outsiders are outsiders, no matter how closely their noses are pressed up against the window looking in. But we became, even in our own minds, Aunt Sue and Uncle Rich. Even our dogs knew us by those names. We spent lots of time with the kids from the start and even more when the Zajacs, the other family to which we had formed ionic bonds, left for Bulgaria. When Harry was still less than a year Richard started having dreams in which Harry talked to him. Stimulating conversations apparently, Richard looked forward to them.

The twins were two, I think, when the new family celebrated their first Christmas in the suburbs. Neither

John nor Mary Beth was religious, and John was made very nervous by any hint that the children might be exposed to any actual real Christianity. But John had passionate feelings about Christmas customs. Artificial trees were sacrilege. Tinsel was essential.

No white Christmas that year, though. We didn't get snow until January, then winter set in for real. Every morning we dug the car out of the snow; every night we tried to get a parking space on the "good side" of the street, the one the snowplows wouldn't have reburied by morning.

One evening I was congratulating myself on getting one of the good parking spaces when the phone rang. It was Mary Beth.

"Susan, you have to come up here right away. I'm taking John to the hospital. We think he has appendicitis. Mom and Dad are here, but . . ."

"I'm on my way."

Between the slushy roads and the rush hour traffic it took over an hour to get over the bridge. Westchester looked like a picture post card, blanketed in snow, the lights shining in the houses.

The volunteer at the desk directed me to a waiting area on the second floor. "They're all there," she said. I followed her directions to the elevator.

The first thing I noticed was a pair of brown paper shopping bags with the "Zabar's" logo. I could smell the potato salad. Then I saw John's father and stepmother, gripping the bags with clenched fists and whitening knuckles. John's stepmother was breathing deeply; his father looked dazed as if he just received a blow to the head.

I looked around for my sister. Mary Beth was sitting in one of the chairs, her hand at her mouth, staring straight ahead.

I forced myself to ask, "What's going on?"

Mary Beth didn't blink; John's father, Jim, shut his eyes as if he were trying very hard to remember something. His wife, Nadine, answered me.

"They found something," she said softly. "A cancerous mass in the colon."

No one had called Lee yet. I got that job. When I got back to the waiting room, a doctor was just finishing explaining next steps to the family. In the morning John would be transferred to Sloan Kettering, the great cancer hospital in Manhattan. The doctor finished and then there was nothing left to do but go home. Still, we didn't move for a while. At the time I did not understand why, but over time watching cancer one learns the games it plays, the havoc it wreaks on the spirit. We didn't want to move because when we stepped out of the hospital back into ordinary life we would bring the cancer with us, where it would be real and undeniable.

"Jim?" I touched John's father's shoulder. "Would you like to come with me?"

He looked at me, still dazed. "We brought a picnic," he whispered. "A picnic."

I slept on my sister's couch that night. In the morning I woke up with a feeling of deep horror in my heart, followed by wild hope—maybe it was all a dream!—followed by even deeper horror: no, that was no dream. It's really happening. It was a pattern we'd get used to.

At the hospital the next day Lee and I sat in the waiting room, waiting.

Finally Lee looked at me, "So, what do you think?"

"About what?"

She gestured vaguely at our surroundings. "This. All this."

I stared straight ahead. "Maybe they're wrong."

"Maybe." She was silent a moment. "What if they're not?"

"This can't happen," I said. "It just can't."

"So you think it won't?"

"It just can't," I repeated. "I don't believe God would do something like this. The kids are still in diapers, for God's sake. He wouldn't do this to us."

Lee looked at me curiously. "You really believe in God, don't you?"

"Yeah. I do."

"Why?"

"Because . . ." I stopped. "Because the world just doesn't make sense to me otherwise."

Lee looked away. "This doesn't make any sense, Susan."

I didn't say anything. She was absolutely right.

ഇ • ൙

I pushed my cart up and down the aisles of the Food Emporium, trying to think what else they needed at the house.

Juice. Lee said to get juice.

But what juice?

Pineapple, papaya, kiwi fruit. Guava. Pineapple-guava. It took ages just to find the shelf with the apple juice, which held also cranberry-apple juice, apple-grape juice, apple-mango, apple-pear, apple-blueberry, apple-strawberry. Cranberry juice was supposed to be good for you; apple juice was rumored to be just sugar; would the twins go for cranberry-apple? Would Harry? Would they all burst into tears because Aunt Sue didn't get the right kind?

"Excuse me." A young woman with her hair in a ponytail and an infant carrier perched in her cart reached past me and plucked a big bottle of juice off the shelf. "Juice, juice, juice," she cooed under her breath as the baby waved a tiny fist in the air. "OK, let's go pay for our juice!" She wheeled her cart around and walked briskly down the aisle, her running shoes squeaking on the polished floor, her ponytail bouncing behind her.

I grabbed a bottle and followed her to the checkout.

The supermarket was right across the street from the Catholic church. The side door was open.

The church was dark and empty except for a guy in gray work clothes, polishing the floor with a machine. The machine hummed softly over the tiles as he pushed it down a side aisle.

I slipped into a pew.

You let my brother die.

You took Sharon.

You didn't give Kasia a green card and now the boys live in stupid Bulgaria.

And you never gave me any babies.

It didn't matter how faithful I was to you. You did it all anyway.

Please let John live. Let him live to see his children grow up. I promise I will never ask you for babies again. And I'll never complain about it again either. I'll never complain about Sharon or Kasia or anything else. But please, don't do this.

Lee came running in to the kitchen. "Oh, thank God, juice." She filled three sippy cups and ran out again.

From the TV room Dean let out a wail. A second later Emma came charging into the kitchen. She shook her sippy cup at us furiously. "Eh! Eh, eh!"

Harry also brought his sippy cup. "Emma says the juice is yucky."

"It's just apple juice," I protested.

Richard picked up the bottle. "Strawberry."

"What?"

"It's apple-strawberry."

"Aunt Sue!" Harry shouted. "Dean is allergic to strawberries!" Lee tore out of the kitchen.

"Richard poured what was left of the juice into the sink.

"Aunt Sue?"

I looked around. Harry was standing beside me.

He patted my hand. "It's all right, Aunt Sue. Everybody makes mistakes sometimes."

XIV

Illness is a world where no one else can follow.
— Flannery O'Connor

ancer is its own world. And the cancer patient enters it alone. No matter how many loving friends and family are around him, no matter how many supporters on the sidelines, the cancer patient embarks upon a journey of suffering unfathomable to the onlookers. It's not just the physical pain. Most of us know pain. Piled on top of the pain is the terrible burden of expectation the disease lays on its victims.

Cancer patients are supposed to "fight back." Why? How? Nobody expects you to "fight back" against leprosy, or a massive heart attack. Or tuberculosis. In nineteenth-century novels tuberculosis patients wither and die decorously and nobody tells them they have to beat this tuberculosis thing. The blind and deaf are urged to cope, maybe even transcend, but nobody expects them to fight off blindness or deafness.

A cancer patient is a civilian one day and a general the next, consulting his advisors, sifting through intelligence reports, hearing of some rumored enemy weakness, or a new super-weapon that just might work, giving or withholding his consent to the attack. Here's the difference. When a real general orders an attack he knows within hours or days whether it's victory or defeat; the cancer general may wait weeks or months and even then victory is never final. More reports from the front drift in, always fragmentary, hedged with pre-varications, fraught with surmise. If a real general finds he is being lied to, he knows the liar for a traitor and an enemy, to be shot at dawn. The cancer general is sur-rounded by liars he loves, or liars he needs. But why are they lying and in which direction? Are they exag-gerating the good news because they want him to fight on, long past his last strength, or are they lying to give him permission to let go? And the doctors. Which way are they shading the truth, even with the best inten-tions? In favor of one more experiment because the dis-covery that it extends life for a month today may mean that someday it will extend life for a year, or against it because their calculus of cost and benefit is not the same as that of a young father with three children at home?

Whom to trust? Whom to believe? And not one has a clue what life is like in this alternate universe, this look-ing-glass war, where of all the instruments of torture the most terrible is hope itself.

I was not an insider in that world. I wasn't even a bit player, really; I was a babysitter, an extra pair of hands, a filler of gaps in someone else's schedule. But whoever said "they also serve who only stand and wait" knew what he was talking about. Especially if by "serving" he meant put every fiber of their being into hope.

Does that surprise you? That I should care so much? OK, let's be blunt. Let's put it as awkwardly and uncomfortably as possible. Who was I anyway? What right did I even have to feel this all so deeply? John was not my husband. He was not even my brother. He was my brother-in-law, for heaven's sake. What's a brother-in-law, to me, to anyone?

Was it about Mary Beth, then? You know, sisters, feeling each other's pain, close in age, almost like twins, growing up together, sharing dreams and heartbreaks?

Gimme a break. We had never been especially close. We had almost nothing in common. Mary, big, busty, loud, full of life, and down to earth, the girl voted most likely to spend her junior prom in the bathroom throwing up drunk. (Prediction fulfilled.)

Me? Well, me.

Like most people who know me well, Mary Beth did not especially like me. She had never hesitated to make this dislike or her disapproval obvious. She had been particularly disdainful over the years about my ambitions as a writer, which she thought all pretentious nonsense. "A snob-wannabe" she called me once, unprovoked by anything that I can remember. She wasn't even angry. Just said it, just like that. For my own good maybe she thought it, or simply to be mean, who knows?

Had Mary known how hard John's sickness all hit me, I think, if anything, she would have been angry, as if somehow I were encroaching on her grief. A snob-wannabe, even in the cancer ward.

I got some hint of this years later. Just at the time John was diagnosed we had been preparing to leave New York. The pressure of making a living freelancing in the city was getting to us both, and Richard had been offered a whole new career at a publishing house in DC. So we packed up and moved to Washington. Two hundred and thirty miles north, however, Mary Beth still needed help. So our life fell into a new pattern. Every couple of weeks John underwent a round of chemotherapy, or some other treatment of the moment. He and MB would spend the night after therapy at his parents' apartment, which was near the hospital. As often as I could I drove—or sometimes flew—up to New York so I could stay with the kids or make myself useful in some way.

It was a big deal for us, for me to be gone that much. Big enough even that after some soul-searching, we'd decided to put the adoption process, which we'd started in our new home in Maryland, on hold, knowing it might be a couple years before everything was resolved with John. Of course I never told Mary Beth about that. But years later, I did mention, at some family gathering, I forget in what context, how often I had made the trip to New York in those years and why.

Mary Beth, standing right there, turned on me with savage sarcasm: "Oh, yeah, Susan, right, you did that," as if I had never done any such thing.

In Mary's defense, I am quite sure she can not remember a fraction of the help any of us tried to give her in those days. She might as well have been in a coma. Everyone was watching her, hyperaware of every look on her face; she couldn't see anyone except John and the kids.

I haven't answered the question. In fact, I'm evading the question. Why did I care so much; what right did I have to care so much?

Part of it, I think, is that, as with the Zajac boys, it's what childless couples do. The ion thing. We bond with unusual ferocity to children and families not our own, often unrealized by the families themselves. Still it was more than that.

OK, this part is really pathetic. I hate writing about it. But their life together. Their wonderful life. The three great kids. Mary Beth, who I'd been longing to see date someone who worked "indoors and unarmed" suddenly with a husband who was smart and funny and loving and successful and a great father. Mary Beth totally transformed, the wild girl became the earth mother. The material stuff, too: the great house in Bronxville, the kids in just the right schools. All of it. So great, so unexpected. And in a big way I had done it. Lee and I, anyway.

Look, it's embarrassing, but I hadn't done anything else. Nothing. List the sum total of my life's accomplishments that actually mattered, and it came down to I set my sister up on the most successful blind date in history. And now what? It gets ripped apart? Mary, devastated; the kids, deprived of wonderful John, deprived so young that as John told me one night, the twins wouldn't even remember him.

All that, yes. But there is one other thing and it doesn't have much to do with me specifically and probably half the people reading this book will not understand it. But it's different for us. I mean believers. "People of faith." The boundaries break down. In the world as seen by believers I wasn't an outsider. I wasn't uninvolved because if God is real no one is uninvolved; no one does just stand and wait. We are linked not just by "feelings" but also by spirit. And spirit is real, more real than anything else, the unseen more factual than the seen.

Love is real. I don't mean the feeling. Who knows if any feeling is real? But when Christians say "God is Love" it's not just a poetic way of saying God is "nice" or God is "sweet" or even that God loves us. It means that this thing that we experience as a feeling, this Hallmark-card sentiment, that the world is actually made of this, that love is the reason the Earth goes around the Sun, that atoms don't fly apart or cease to exist.

The mystical body of Christ. I am Christ and you are Christ and we all are a part of His body not as a bit of poetry but part of Him as really and truly as His presence in the Host is real and true and by our communion with Him all sons and daughters of the same Father.

Look, I don't care if you think it is ridiculous. It's how we live. And it means that nothing is without meaning, nothing is unconnected, nothing and no one is outside the story.

Above all, it means that we pray. And it means that prayer is not just hope expressed, but an event in the universe, a message from spirit to spirit ten thousand times more real than anything FedEx ever delivered (not to mention the Italian post office).

So there it is. Say he was just my brother-in-law, that it wasn't my battle, there was nothing I could do, but in the universe in which I live I was fighting hard for John and Mary Beth and that beautiful little family, fighting harder than any doctor every time I got down on my knees.

OK, go ahead, all you skeptics, all you intellectuals, all you cutting-edge cocktail-party atheists. Time to laugh.

Go to hell.

XV

Besides. I had connections.

In August 1910, Francesco Forgione, a young Italian man of peasant stock, was ordained to the priesthood, taking the name Padre Pio in religious life. Barely a month later, Padre Pio was deep in prayer when he had a mystical vision of Christ with his mother, the Virgin Mary. It was during this experience that two small wounds appeared on his hands for the first time.

The stigmata—from the Greek "stigma," meaning a mark or a brand, like the ones on cattle—are the wounds of the crucified Christ appearing in the body of a human being. The first recorded instance of the stigmata occurred in 1224, when Francis of Assisi received the wounds as he was praying on Mount Averna.

There are different kinds of stigmata. Some, like those of St. Francis, are visible to anyone who can get close enough to look. Others like those borne by St. Catherine of Siena and St. Teresa of Avila are invisible—the stigmatist feels all the pain of the wounds but shows no external signs of them.

When he first received the stigmata Padre Pio was appalled not so much by the pain, which was intense, as by the spectacle. He immediately went to the parish priest of his hometown and begged him to ask God to take the wounds away. The two priests prayed, and the marks disappeared. The pain, however, remained.

Eight years later the wounds appeared again on his feet and hands. This time they did not disappear. Within a year the story had spread throughout the countryside. When a newspaper in Naples published a story about the "saint," Pio's life was changed forever. The monastery of San Giovannni Rotondo, where he lived, became a pilgrimage site, visited by the faithful from all over the world.

Official reaction from the Church ranged from skeptical to hostile. In 1923, a Vatican inquiry led to a decree from the "Holy Office"—yes, gentle reader, that is the "Inquisition"—declaring that "an inquiry on the phenomena of Padre Pio of Pietrelcina" was unable to confirm "any basis for the supernatural character of these phenomena and exhorts the faithful to conform their practices to this declaration."

Skepticism soon became persecution. The archbishop of Foggia declared Pio was "possessed" and the monks of his monastery a gang of swindlers. In July of 1924 the Holy Office issued a condemnation urging the faithful "to abstain from any kind of contact, even by letter, with the above-named priest." Pio was placed under restrictions that amounted to house arrest. He was forbidden to say public masses, make any public appearances, or even go down to the monastery parlor. But when a rumor began to go round that Pio was to be removed to another monastery the citizens of Pietrelcina rose up and mobbed the gates of the monastery. Pio stayed.

Eventually the restrictions on Padre Pio were lifted though the official Church remained skeptical. All the time the stories multiplied. Padre Pio's prayers were said to save crops, heal the sick, and even once to stop a bocce ball in mid-flight. (The ball had been about to hit a cat.) Crippled children walked; cancers were dispatched; a little girl born without pupils gained her sight. Penitents who slipped into Pio's confessional were frequently shocked to hear the monk recount their life stories for them, warts and all. Pio was reputed to have the gift of bi-location, to be in two places at once. During the Second World War, an American bomber squadron stationed at Bari was sent to destroy a German munitions dump near San Giovanni Rotondo. As they approached they suddenly saw the figure of a bearded monk, hands upraised, warning them away. At that moment the bombs broke loose by themselves and fell, destroying the correct target without hitting the monastery. After the war some of the pilots went to visit San Giovanni Rotondo. Padre Pio took one look at them and said, "So! You're the ones who wanted to destroy everything!"

Of all the stories, however, only one interested me.

In 1947 a young Polish priest traveled to San Giovanni Rotondo where he met and spoke with Padre Pio. Fifteen years later that priest, now bishop of Kraków, sent an urgent message to Pio through a Vatican emissary. Translated from the Latin the message read:

Venerable Father,

I ask you to pray for a certain mother of four girls, who lives in Kraków, Poland (during the last war she spent five years in a concentration camp in Germany), and now she finds herself in a very grave danger of health, even of life because of cancer. Pray so that the Lord, with the intervention of the Most Blessed Virgin, may show mercy to her and to her family.

Most obligated in Christ,

+Karol Wojtyla.

The emissary who delivered the letter to Padre Pio at his monastery in November 1962 was baffled. He had been told the letter was of maximum importance, yet except for coming from a Polish bishop about whom none of his colleagues in the Vatican knew anything of interest, it seemed no different from hundreds of requests the monk received every day.

Padre Pio was silent as the letter was read aloud to him. He bent his head in prayer, then looked at the emissary. "To this one," he said, "one cannot say no."

Eleven days later the emissary returned with a second letter:

Venerable Father,

The woman living in Kraków, Poland, the mother of four girls, on November 21, before the surgery, was healed unexpectedly. Let us thank God. And also to you, Venerable Father, I offer you the greatest thanks in the name of the same woman, her husband, and her entire family.

In Christ,

+Karol Wojtyla, Capitular Bishop of Kraków

"Save the letters," the monk instructed. "One day they will be important."

Padre Pio died in 1968. The cause for his canonization was taken up in 1983, two years after that bishop of Kraków was elected pope. The "certain mother of four girls" was *La Dottoressa*, Kasia's mother.

As part of a "cause" or case for canonization the canon lawyer advocating canonization must present overwhelming evidence for at least two miracles performed through the intercession of the candidate for sainthood. (Saints don't "perform" miracles: God does. The saints just ask.) The *Advocatus Diaboli*—the devil's advocate—the lawyer opposing the case will do everything in his lawful power to disprove the claim. *La Dottoressa* was one of Pio's miracles.

I wanted to add another.

Pio saved *La Dottoressa* because she had four children to raise. John had three. And they were beautiful, beautiful children. And John was a wonderful man and a wonderful father. My sister and he were so happy together. Karol Wojtyla asked Padre Pio to save one family and he did it, just like that. He could do it again. He could, he could, he could.

Dear Kasia,
    Of course we are coming to Italy this summer! We will be staying at the Bucci—can't wait to see you. Oh, and there's one other thing . . .

XVI

Summer came. John bought the kids a wading pool and set it up in the backyard. I continued coming up to New York as scheduled, to watch the kids splash around while he and MB spent a couple of days doing things like signing their wills and seeing more doctors.

One warm day I was sitting poolside, finally reading a book Sharon had sent me, *Miracles Do Happen*, when Harry scrambled out of the pool and ran over to me, dripping wet. "Aunt Sue, can I ask you something?"

"Sure, Harry."

"How come you're always here?"

"What?" I put the book down. "I'm not always here. I mean, I'm here a lot, but . . ."

Oh, God. What was I going to say now? I'm here so your daddy can get his chemotherapy?

"No, no." Harry waved his hands dismissively. "I mean, if you're here, who's taking care of your kids?"

"Um, I don't have kids, honey."

His eyes flew open. "No kids?"

"Nope. No kids."

He clicked his tongue sympathetically and laid a thoughtful finger to his lips. He frowned in thought. "Get a kiddie pool."

"Dad-DEEEEE! Mom-MEEEEE!" Emma clambered out of the pool and hurled herself, dripping, into her mother's arms. I stashed my book under a pillow.

"Hi, Em! Have a good swim?" Mary Beth grabbed a towel and rubbed her daughter's head briskly. "Mamma mia. You're a wrinkly little raisin! You're a prune! How long have they been in the water, Aunt Sue?"

"Dean's been in and out, but Emma's been in the water for about two hours, I think."

"That's my little water rat," John beamed. "Kid's gonna be an Olympic swimmer."

Emma sneezed. "Kid's going to catch pneumonia," MB muttered. "Come on, Em. Let's go get a snack. Anybody else hungry?"

The kids followed her into the house.

John sat down and stretched out in the sun. "So how was your day, Aunt Sue?"

"It was great." I covered a yawn. "A little exhausting."

Then he saw the book. "You're not reading this to Harry, are you?"

"Of course not."

"Good. Because they don't, you know."

"You're going to get well, John," I said quietly.

John glanced over his shoulder toward the house.

Mary Beth was safely inside. He turned back to me.

"No," he whispered. "I'm not. Look, I've read every-thing there is to read about this stuff. When I was diag-nosed for the first time I already had Stage IV colon cancer. I'll be dead before the twins are old enough to remember me. "And that," he gestured toward my book, "is a lot of crap."

The screen door opened behind us. Mary Beth came out with a tray. John shot me a meaningful look. *Don't say a thing; she's not ready.*

"Anybody want some iced tea?"

In the kitchen we made hamburger patties. "Porto-bello mushrooms?" I asked. "Will the kids eat them?"

"Harry will. We've been eating a lot of vegetables since John got sick. The grill helps. John loves it." She pulled out a cookbook. "Where's that marinade? . . . OK. I need lemon juice."

I looked over my shoulder. My sister was standing in front of the open refrigerator, holding a package of luncheon meat in her hand. She was practically shaking with anger.

"Look at this. Look at this! 'Salami for beer.' He's been buying it again. He promised me! He has can-cer, for God's sake! And he's eating this? Nitrates and chemicals and God knows what else, and I'm trying to keep him healthy and keep the kids happy and pretend everything's normal and we can handle this . . ."

She sank to the floor and buried her head in her hands. "Oh, God. Oh, my God . . ."

We heard a car in the driveway. My sister jumped up and dashed to the sink. She shoved her face under the tap.

"Got the asparagus! Got the mushrooms, got some ice pops . . ." John looked at his wife. "Oh, Mary Beth. You're not doing that crazy ice water thing again?"

She kept her head underwater, waving a hand at her husband.

"Oh, for pity's sake. She read in some magazine that sticking her face in ice water for five minutes a day will keep her skin looking younger." He stuck his head into the sink and yelled in her ear. "Where's your snorkel? I bought you a snorkel. Harry! Where's Mommy's snorkel?"

"In the kiddie pool!"

The screen door banged shut.

Mary Beth lifted her head out of the sink. She dried her face with a paper towel. "Lemons," she repeated huskily. "I need two." And she went back to work, juicing lemons and mixing her marinade, as if nothing had happened.

There was pile of photographs scattered on the dining room table. I picked up a Polaroid of John and the three kids. "Can I have this picture?" I called.

"Yeah, sure, we have a ton of them."

I put the Polaroid in my purse.

XVII

Up at dawn again. The mountain air cool and lovely as we slipped out of the hotel. Once again the town felt empty as we walked up the narrow streets to the palace. We passed one dimly lit shop open for coffee and morning pastries; inside a woman with long red hair tied back in a ponytail chatted with a police officer while she ran the espresso machine. She caught my gaze as I passed and gave me a smile. I gave her a nervous smile in return.

I kept sticking my hand into my purse. The photo was still there. Exactly where it was the last time I checked, ten or twenty seconds ago.

I kept trying to come up with a script in my head. "Holy Father, this is my sister's husband." No, make that "this is my brother-in-law. He's very sick." No, be specific. Say he has cancer. "These are his children; see how young they are? Well, actually, this picture is a year old; they're a lot bigger now." No, leave that out; he'll get the point. "Holy Father, this is my brother-in-law. He's sick; he has cancer. Please pray for him." No, something stronger. "I'm begging you. Ask God to make him well.

He is such a wonderful man; you'd love him. And you'd love these kids too; they're so much fun, and they love their father so much." Richard knocked at the gate.

"Giorno." A Swiss Guard saluted and handed us over not to the security detail or the little monsignor but to Stan who with no ceremony to prepare for was free to meet us. Compared to our earlier breakneck tear, this morning's walk through the palace corridors was a leisurely stroll. Stan kept pointing things out along the way. "See that ramp over there? That was built for donkey carts. For luggage, you know."

"You may have noticed the bees on this coat of arms: Urban VIII was a Barberini; the bees are their symbol, of course. The boys call them 'the killer bees.'"

"Our apartment is over that way. During the war it was always full of refugees." (During the war, the summer palace sheltered more Jews from the Nazis than any other single site in Axis Europe. So much for "Hitler's Pope.")

I scarcely heard him. "Dear God," I prayed, "whatever else happens, please don't let me lose my nerve. I don't care how bad I look; I don't care if *La Dottoressa* yells at me and calls me a pushy American in front of everyone; I'll take whatever she hands out; but please, please don't let me lose my nerve."

Once again Holy Father was kneeling on a simple prie-dieu in the aisle, deep in prayer, oblivious to everything around him. Once again at some unheard signal he roused himself and got slowly to his feet. An assistant helped him into his vestments; a couple of other priests appeared on the altar; the mass began.

The Catholic Church teaches that the Eucharist, the consecrated Host that is distributed at mass, is The Real Thing: really Christ's flesh, really Christ's body.

It's not an easy concept. For centuries theologians have struggled to explain it. For me it always seemed pretty straightforward, if for no other reason than whom Christ chose to share Himself with. He knew the apostles intimately; he loved them. He also knew they weren't exactly a brain trust. And He knew He was going to die in a few hours. I could never believe that He would choose that moment to screw around with metaphors. So I take Him at his word. "This bread, this wine? This is really Me."

As the assisting priests handed out Communion — once again the pope did not distribute — I thought about what a great equalizer the Eucharist was. There are all sorts of people in the Catholic Church: rich, poor; well connected, friendless; powerful, powerless. But to receive the Eucharist the requirements are the same for everyone: be in a state of grace and when your turn comes, make a simple affirmation. "Body of Christ," the priest says. "Amen," the communicant responds: yes, I believe it. I believe this outlandish, impossible, unfathomable thing.

When everyone who had lined up had received, the pope sat back in his chair and propped his chin on his fist, gazing thoughtfully into the congregation.

The chapel was full. Kasia and her family were in the first pews opposite us again, just as they had been at the First Communion and the Confirmation two years before. The rows behind them were filled with people I didn't recognize. Friends of Kasia's parents, perhaps, or more of the pope's old friends from home. The first rows on our side of the aisle were once again filled with nuns. Maybe those are the nun rows. Maybe whenever a bunch of sisters from out of town come to the pope's private mass they get the front-row seats.

Unlike Sharon's, this order wore "modern" habits. Modern in the case of nuns' habits is not a synonym for fashionable. Short skirts, polyester blazers, skimpy black veils perched on the backs of their heads. Very K-Mart.

The Holy Father completed his meditation and stood up. Everyone else stood up with him. The final blessings were said, and the mass was over. The priests left the altar; the congregation filed outside.

The long, wide gallery where we waited was lined with windows. The crowd split up into three or four different groups: the nuns off in their own little cluster, Kasia's mother and her guests in another, Richard and me together.

Kasia came over, smiling. "I was just talking to my

father. He didn't recognize you, Susan. He said you looked much better than you did the last time. Apparently staying out of the hospital does wonders for you."

"Thanks. I guess."

Walter was giggling. "One time Holy Father did not recognize Aunt Sharon. She was crushed. He remembered her later, though. He said, 'Oh yes, she got a new hairdo.'"

"She made sure she kept her hair the same the next summer," Stan added.

A door opened and a handful of people burst into applause. John Paul II smiled and started making the rounds.

"Did you bring the picture?" Kasia whispered.

"It's right here."

"Good. You must show it to him."

I was resolved, but at the last minute I decided that getting the message across clearly was more important than me overcoming my own shyness. "No, you do it, please. You'll make him understand."

My turn. I said hello, kissed the ring, and looked meaningfully at Kasia.

Kasia touched the pope's arm. "Holy Father? May I show you —" she produced the picture and started speaking in soft but rapid Polish. I watched as her finger passed over the glossy paper, hovering above the faces of my family. The pope was following closely, frowning and nodding as she told him the story. His gaze lingered on the picture even after Kasia had finished her story.

He looked at me and nodded. Kasia was still talking, still in Polish, and I had no idea what she was saying. But the pope was looking at me as if we were old and dear friends, and he was just as concerned as I was about the little family Kasia was telling him about. He turned to the assistant who always follows behind on these occasions carrying a tray of rosaries that the pope has blessed, gifts for his guests. He picked up a rosary from the tray and handed it to me with a solemn nod. Then he turned back to the assistant again and plucked another from the tray. He handed this one to me, too, touching my hand with both of his as he did so.

Then the audience was over. The pope held up his hands as he stood by the door one of the other priests was holding for him. He blessed the crowd and turned away. Everyone clapped.

Everyone was still clapping when he suddenly stopped. He turned around and walked across the gallery to me. He touched my hand, looked me in the eye, and said, "John?"

"Yes," I nodded eagerly. "John. His name is John."

He nodded and touched my hand one last time. Then he was gone.

XVIII

There were stretches of days, even weeks when John seemed to be getting better. His hair grew back, completely white now but as full as ever. He went to work every day.

By now he had a whole new set of doctors. He was admitted to a program that was experimenting with new and ever more exotic treatments. A "port" was surgically implanted in his chest, so he could take new intravenous meds. Of course he loved showing it off. "Right here. Go ahead, put your hand right here. Cool, huh? Susan! Have you seen this?"

John took the children sledding in the winter and to the beach in the summer. He taught Harry computer games and built the twins a little fort in the backyard. It had to come down when Emma could not be deterred from climbing to the top and dropping rocks on her brother's head. There was even a trip to Disney World in the spring. Long lines, subtropical rainstorms, and insanely overpriced treats are bad enough when a man is feeling at his best; I could not imagine what it was like for a man with a chronic illness and in more or less constant pain.

At Thanksgiving John was feeling so well that the

family decided to drive to DC. Lee, Mary Beth, and I rotated Thanksgiving hostess duty in those years and it was Aunt Lee's turn.

Lee's and Bill's house tucked away in a beautiful old Northern Virginia suburb overlooked a lake. The entire back of the house was walled with windows; every room had a lake view. Right behind the house was a deck with a fire pit and a hot tub; several terraces below were a boat dock and a small boat.

"Can we go see the boat? Aunt Sue says Aunt Lee has a boat!"

"We can't take it out on the lake, Harry," Lee said. "It's not licensed."

"Could we just sit in it?"

Lee looked at my sister. She shrugged. "All right. But wear a lifejacket."

"Yay!" The twins ran for the dock, Emma in the lead. Aunt Lee followed, shouting precautions as she picked her way down the stairs.

John grimaced. Mary Beth frowned.

"What's wrong? Are you all right?"

"I'm fine. Just a little twinge."

"You shouldn't be drinking Coke."

A brief look of exasperation flashed across his face. "I know that, Mary Beth. I shouldn't be drinking Coke, or coffee, or beer, or anything but what? The purest mountain spring water? For God's sake, it's Thanksgiving."

My sister pressed her lips together and said nothing.

A tense silence fell. It didn't last.

What happened next remains a subject of some debate. Some say it was all Deanie's fault, others finger Emma, still others say Aunt Lee really should have seen it coming. At any rate, our tense silence was broken by the sound of a shriek, a splash, and then . . . the laughter of little children.

Twenty minutes later, Bill cleared his throat. "Well, dear, at least we know the hot tub works."

Lee scowled. For someone sitting in a Jacuzzi with a single-malt scotch in her hand she still looked pretty miffed.

"I should have brought my suit," John mused. "That looks pleasant."

"It wasn't pleasant in the lake," she snapped. "That water's freezing."

"Well, it is November," Richard said helpfully. Lee shot him a look. "Um—why don't I go inside and build a nice fire?"

"Good idea. I'll help." The guys all jumped up and went into the house. Mary Beth and the kids were already hiding inside for fear of busting out laughing in front of Aunt Lee.

Lee sipped her scotch. After a moment she looked up. "He looks good, don't you think?"

"Oh, yeah. I like his new doctors."

She turned her gaze to the lake. "He has some tests coming up."

"When?"

"In about two weeks. Middle of December. That's when they'll know."

XIX

Dear Sue,

Happy Advent! They put me in charge of the wreath. For once I got my act together early and have everything in place. Although whoever thought of purple and pink candles in the same arrangement clearly was not thinking of our chapel. Really clashes. Oh well.

Still, it's lovely to have some pink in my life! Remember those tulips I was so addicted to, the deep pink with the white tips? I still miss them. And my pink Dior dress . . . Sigh.

By the way, I, too, have had to fight the "maybe it's none of my business" thing. You're never sure if you're being respectful or cowardly in these situations. Keep praying to the Spirit for guidance. He won't let you down, I promise.

Gotta go. Love to all,

Sharon (Sister Stephen!)

On the morning of John's test results I was too excited to do anything but go Christmas shopping. So I headed over to Union Station, all but a ruin when I first came to Washington after college, but by then, with its grand old interior, reborn as an upscale shopping arcade, including one store devoted entirely to Thomas the Tank Engine.

I was going for it. I was getting Harry and Dean the biggest and best Thomas accessory of all, The Round House, along with various special tracks and accessories to go with it, all of hand-painted wood. One serious outlay of holiday cash.

I cared not. I hummed to myself as I glided down the escalator. Christmas music blasted over the sound system, echoing off the marble floors and the glassed-in storefronts. The mall was packed with shoppers and their full-to-bursting shopping bags. It was Christmas, the time of hope and wild commerce. It was beautiful.

At eleven AM Eastern time John and my sister would be in his doctor's office, getting the test results. They'd be home by noon, and then I could call. I had just enough time.

I found my way to the Thomas shop and told a woman in a striped apron what I needed. She led me to an elaborate display. "Amazing, isn't it?"

"Amazing," I agreed. "I'll take it."

"All right. Is there someone here to help you?"

"Sorry?"

"The box is very heavy. You'll need some help carrying it."

"No, I'm here alone. But don't worry," I said cheerfully. "I can manage."

She wasn't kidding; the carton weighed a ton. But the holiday spirit was strong with me that morning, and I hoisted the box and got it out the door. I checked my watch: nearly noon.

A brass band played "Good King Wenceslas." No way I could carry the box all through the mall, so I began sliding it along the polished stone floor, looking for a pay phone. Halfway to the other end of the mall I found one.

Sharon always said, "Be grateful in advance. Show God you trust Him." I shoved the coins through the slot with a flourish of gratitude. Oh, God, thank you, thank you, thank you for this wonderful day, this beautiful season! Thank you for getting John the best medical help in the world! Thanks for hope, hope, hope abundant!

"Hello."

"Mary Beth? It's me! So, what's the good word?"

It was impossible to hear her above the noise.

"What? I'm in Union Station. I can barely hear you!"

"I said the liver, Susan! It's spread to the liver!" The line went dead.

XX

Dear Sharon,

Happy New Year—many weeks late, obviously. I'm sorry I haven't written in so long.

John is very sick. I don't know what, if anything, the new treatments are doing for him. He never talks about it, and my sister doesn't either, at least not to me. All they ever say about the treatments is "they're very aggressive."

Every time I see John he's thinner and weaker. You can imagine what my sister looks like.

Love,

S.

Dear Kasia,

Here's a question: What the hell use is a "test of faith" if the person suffering doesn't have any faith to begin with?

I just talked to Sharon. It's Sunday. She's allowed to take phone calls. She kept telling me how John's illness is a "test of faith." Which seems kind of stupid, given that John doesn't believe in

God. Does God actually think that giving a young husband and father a deadly disease will make him think, "Oh, gosh, the Christians must be right; there is a God and He really loves me!"? Can God possibly be that stupid? Does He think John is?

S.

Dear Sharon,

Happy Easter to you too. Ours was pretty low-key this year. We did have a pretty wild Seder, though. John's father wanted the children to have one with the family. When we got to the questions the twins decided it was riddle time. I've never really thought of "why did the chicken cross the road?" as a response to "why is this night different from all other nights?" but I suppose it makes some sense.

Did you know of all the "Judaica" shops in Scarsdale not one sells yarmulkes? Neither did I, but I know it for a fact now.

John is not good. Neither is MB.

Love,

S.

Dear Kasia,

The children keep asking when is Daddy going to come downstairs, and we keep saying, "Maybe later, let Daddy rest, he's just a little tired right now." The twins may be buying it, but Harry isn't. This past week I have seen a look in my nephew's eyes that no one should ever, ever see in the eyes of a kid his age.

S.

Dear Sharon,

My dear brother-in-law, John, died last night at around one o'clock. His wife and his sister were with him. The children were able to say good-bye.

S.

Dear Sharon,

I would have to say we're still in shock here. That seems strange, given how long it all dragged out. But we walk around dazed, still not believing it. Shock.

One minute my niece will be saying Daddy is gone and we're never going to see him again, like she's reciting a lesson, the next she'll be asking is Daddy going to meet us in East Hampton next week.

My sister is amazing. Every day she gets up and keeps things going for the kids: breakfast, play, visit Grandma, go to the park. It's only after the children have brushed their teeth and gone to bed that she falls apart.

She has been going to a "bereavement group," which she says is helping a little. The other day we were in the supermarket, and she touched my sleeve and pointed. There was an older man in a barber's smock standing in front of the meat case, just running his hands through his hair. "His wife died a month ago," she told me. "Look at him. He doesn't even know how to buy dinner without her. Have you ever seen a total stranger and really felt like your heart could just break for him?"

She tells me the grocery store is a popular place for such breakdowns. Once she ran out and left a cart full of stuff in the dairy aisle—she said she saw the words "expiration date" on a carton and suddenly felt sick.

S.

Dear Kasia,

Thank you for your sweet letter. You were right about the exhaustion—my sister finally came down with pneumonia. So she's finally being forced to get some rest.

We will try to come to Italy this summer.

Love,

Susan

PART IV
Be Not Afraid

XXI

"That looks good," I whispered, being as obvious as possible.

"It is," Kasia smiled teasingly, then handed me what remained of her dessert. "Here, take it. I'm stuffed."

It was Friday night. Every Friday night of the summer vacation, shortly before dark, Pope John Paul II would appear on his balcony. Below him in the courtyard the crowd would burst into cheers. Then after a short introduction, he would take out his rosary, make the sign of the cross, and lead everyone in the ancient prayers.

The Friday Night Rosary had neither the formality of the morning masses in the courtyard nor the excited, party-on atmosphere of the Sunday Angelus. There weren't a lot of tourists or pilgrimage groups around; people from the town would stroll through the gates, waving to their friends on the palace staff or nodding to their neighbors. I had seen the owners of the Bucci here a few times, their rosaries dangling from their fingers as they chatted with their fellow innkeepers. Conversation would mostly cease after the pope began the Apostles' Creed, but even then the staccato of the Latin prayers was interspersed with the whispered flowing Italian of local gossip. It was as if everyone, the pope included, had agreed that, yes, it is the rosary with the pope, but let's not forget it's Friday night. I have never seen a clearer picture of God being part of your whole life, including your night off.

The other difference was that mass and the Angelus went off like clockwork, but the Friday Night Rosary never started on time. The rosary was supposed to start right after dinner. But dinners at the summer palace were notorious gabfests, especially if any of the pope's philosophy professor pals were around. John Paul would get so involved in the conversation he would lose all track of time. Every Friday it was the same: everyone sitting around the table having a blast, the poor nuns finally managing to get the desserts out, and suddenly the pope would look at his watch. "Oh, look at the time! I should be leading the rosary right now! No, please, stay and enjoy your coffee. I'll be right back." Then he would get up from the table. At that, of course, every-one else would jump up, too, scarfing down the last of their cannolis as they ran down to the courtyard. Some-times the boys would remember to snatch a few extra desserts for us, though sometimes the temptation to finish off the loot was too strong. Charlie liked to taunt me with descriptions of the evening's goodies. "It had chocolate chips and lots of cream and it was so yummy, Aunt Susan, . . . Oh, I'm sorry, haven't you had dinner yet? What a shame . . ."

Kasia waved to someone at one of the upper windows. "There's Bishop C. We are supposed to go with him to Rome tomorrow. My mother wants us to be his guides."

"So you won't be around tomorrow?"

"No, nor Sunday either, I'm afraid. I've worked out something for Monday. But it's a surprise."

"Tell me!"

She laughed and stuck out her tongue. "Oh, good, here is Holy Father."

It was after nine and nearly full dark but the pope's white cassock and broad, beaming smile shone from the balcony. The crowd burst into cheers as he raised his hands, greeting and blessing everyone in the courtyard. Even with the noise I could make out Richard bellowing behind us, "Viva il papa!"

The pope raised his hand to his forehead. "In nomine Patris, et Filii . . ."

I would not have guessed, back when I was a gray-skirted, white-shirted schoolgirl, that it would ever be a relief to hear Latin again. But it was. I love Italian, but I understand only a little, and even that is work. On an evening like this I was especially happy to be able to turn off my mental translator.

". . . iudicare vivos et mortuos."

"Credo in Spiritum Sanctum, sanctam ecclesiam catholicam . . . ," the crowd murmured along.

The pope switched to Italian just to announce the

mysteries. "Il primo mistero doloroso, l'agonia di Gesù nell' orto del Getsemani." Then, reassuringly, back to Latin: "Pater noster, qui es in caelis, sanctificetur nomen tuum . . ."

One Our Father, ten Hail Marys, to meditate on Jesus's last hour as a free man, praying in the garden of Gethsemani, sick with fear, begging the Father to please find some other way to accomplish what He had to accomplish.

The Father turned Him down. Sorry, but you're going to have to be tortured to death.

But John's torture went on longer and left my sister and her three children alone.

"Il secondo mistero doloroso, la flagellazione di Gesù alla colonna." The Scourging at the Pillar. Pilate's little gamble. "Maybe if I just almost kill him that will be enough for this mob, and they'll let me go back to the office in peace." But nothing short of an execution would satisfy the people that day.

At least Pilate tried. He tried to let an innocent man get away alive.

I pretended to sneeze so I could dash the tears from my eyes. I needn't have worried; it was too dark now for Kasia to see.

"Ave Maria, gratia plena . . ."

"Sancta Maria, Mater Dei, ora pro nobis peccatoribus . . ." In my own ears my accent stood out like a sore thumb. Even in Latin I sounded like an American, harsh and nasal against the mellifluous Mediterranean backdrop.

"Il terzo mistero, la coronazione di spine. Pater Noster, qui es in caelis . . ."

The third mystery, the Crowning with Thorns. Adding insult to injury. A universal human vice—the urge to kick someone when he's down. "Death with dignity." Ha. Show me the dignity in death.

Afterward my sister told me that John never resigned himself to death. Up until the last possible second he fought it off, believing he would get well if only because he had to, because he had three children to raise. Hours before he slipped into the final coma he was still struggling, using the last of his strength to heave himself out of bed and tumble to the floor, insisting that he had to get up, he had to get dressed, he had better things to do than die. Nearly his last words to Mary Beth were "don't let me die." Where was the dignity in that?

It's all nonsense about those who live on being the ones who really suffer, at least it is when it is a parent dying. I've loved two people who died slowly and who for months or years while waiting to die knew they were abandoning their children. There is no peaceful acceptance of such a death. They both died in sadness and anger and unutterable regret. The greatest saint in heaven would rail against the injustice.

"La salita di Gesù al calvario carico della croce."

"Take up your cross and follow Me." It sounded so noble, until you realized you didn't have any choice. Jesus had a choice. Where was John's?

La Crocifissione.

Of the three men executed that day Jesus died first. Crucifixion is death by asphyxiation; the condemned die from the struggle to catch one more breath. Whenever some poor wretch seemed to be taking too long the Romans would break his legs, so he couldn't push himself up anymore in the struggle to breathe. Jesus was already dead, so there was no need to smash his bones to splinters.

It's a gruesome death.

But it's over in a day. John suffered for years and in so many ways my sister's suffering was just beginning.

"Susan? Are you all right?" Kasia asked.

"What?" It was dark now, and the rosary was finished. The pope had retired from the balcony, and the people were leaving the courtyard, tucking their beads back into their pockets, chatting with their friends in conversations that had started years before. "Yes, I'm, I'm fine. I'm just, you know. A little jet lagged." I tried to laugh. "And hungry."

"I'm afraid the Bucci is closed. I just saw the cook."

"Oh, dear. Richard will be disappointed."

"Listen, I've got to go. Why don't you drive down to the lake? There are plenty of cafés still open there. And have a glass of wine. You look as if you could use it."

"So I'll see you Monday?"

"Yes. I will leave a message at the Bucci." She gave me a quick hug. "Good night."

There was to be a rowing competition on the lake that weekend and Castel Gandolfo was already filling up. All the café tables on the piazza were taken; the music from the bars tucked behind San Tommaso was loud. We stopped in one to grab a slice of pizza and walked slowly back to our hotel. A man in paint-spattered clothes was pasting a huge poster to a wall with a brush. *Epigrafe*. A death notice.

We sat on our balcony for a while, gazing at the lake and listening to the holidaymakers' racket. "You know what?" Richard said at last. "The Zajacs are busy until Monday. There's nothing to keep us in town. What do you say we take off, do a little touring? We can keep our room here. We'll just look at a map and go, first thing in the morning."

"What if Kasia calls?"

"You know she won't. Her mother's calling the shots this weekend. The lake will be crowded; the restaurants will be packed. Let's just look at a map and take off. Take a vacation from our vacation, as you used to say?"

The bell down at the railroad track clanged noisily. Up at the Castelvecchio the night's reigning DJ jacked up the volume on some Italian rap, an odd genre indeed.

"All right," I said. "Let's go. Let's have an adventure."
Richard nodded. "We'll leave right after breakfast."

The next morning while Richard poured over a map
I went to a shop and bought some things for a picnic:
bread, cheese, peaches, *acqua minerale*. "I've got it all
figured out," Richard announced when I returned. "You
drive, I'll navigate."

Since Richard does not like to drive and I can't read
a map to save my life, this is our usual division of labor.

We had decided to spend the weekend in Umbria,
the province east of Tuscany and northeast of Rome,
the province of Assisi, one of our favorite places, and
Deruta, the center of the Italian ceramics industry. We
took a wandering route. I think we lunched in Orvi-
eto, in front of the Duomo. It was closed for siesta, but
that only meant we had to picnic gazing at the gorgeous
mosaic façade on a beautiful summer day. We went
shopping in Deruta where my elementary Italian proved
sufficient to find a little place to stay for the night a few
miles to the south. We got directions and we were feeling our way there when we had our one moment of real
alarm. The sun had begun to set when Richard suddenly
pointed up into the dry hills in front of us. "Oh, my God,
is that a fire?"

Yes! No.

A series of letters burned brightly on a hillside.
"FESTA."

"There's a feast," I said. "Somewhere up there."

"Let's go find it!"

We drove up into the hills.

By the time we found the town it was nearly full dark, and the feast was in full swing. Booths sold zeppoli and soda pop and chances to win big stuffed animals. Carnival rides were set up in a field. Music was everywhere, as bands for the young and old competed for attention.

With the help of a couple of high school kids who spoke reasonably good English we learned that it was not only the Feast of San Lorenzo, patron of the local church, but the town's annual vin santo festival to celebrate the latest vintage of the Italian dessert wine made in the region. There were special booths set up where you could buy a glass. "But that is for dessert," one kid told us. "First you eat. See? Over there."

Picnic tables were set up in rows under a tent. It was astonishing how much food our tickets bought us. Soup, pasta, meat, salad—it just kept coming. All delicious. The dinner tickets were cheap, around seven dollars apiece, but they did not include any vin santo. That turned out to be the real money maker, as a glass of the chilled wine and two biscotti cost almost as much as a whole dinner. Worth every penny.

Whump. Whump. Whump. Beyond the cooking tents someone was testing a microphone. Richard and I followed the crowd. A stage and a dance floor had been set up under the open sky. While the band was setting up, pop music played over the loudspeakers. Couples drifted onto the floor.

"Wanna dance?" Richard asked.

"You know I can't dance."

"That doesn't seem to be stopping anyone else," he shouted as the sound of pulsing bass and a synthesizer took over the night. "Hey! I know this one!"

I had to laugh. "It's that thing they do at the ball park. The Macarena!"

"All right! Come on!"

What can I say? I was in a little town in central Italy where nobody knew me, I was on vacation, and I'd had two glasses of *vin santo*. I went out onto the dance floor with my husband and did the Macarena. Twice.

Later as we walked back over the fields to our rental car Richard stopped to gape at the sky. "Look at that."

You know you're out in the country when the night sky is so jammed with stars it looks bright even with a new moon. I had no idea where Rome was from here, or Castel Gandolfo.

Richard smiled, reading my mind. "Don't worry, I know the way back."

"Mm. That's almost too bad."

We walked to the car in silence. More marital mind reading. "Give it time," he said. "Mary Beth will start to get better, so will the kids. They'll build a new life . . ."

"But their old life was great," I said bitterly.

XXI

He had no answer to that. I just kept my hands on the wheel and drove through the pitch black hills, waiting for directions, taking it on faith.

XXII

onday morning the lady who ran the Bucci handed me a note. "Signora Vigilante? A message for you."

"Grazie." I slipped the note out of the envelope.

Susan—Come to the piazza at ten. Your surprise will be waiting. Love, Kasia.

"Oh, my God!" I shrieked the second I saw them. I ran across the square. "What are you doing here?"

"I'm always here!" Sharon's wide linen sleeves swallowed me up in a big hug. "There's no party without me."

We made a plan for the day—after lingering at the piazza over coffee and cornetti—to spend a few hours in the gardens: no fear of disturbing Holy Father who had to be in Rome that day. We were to be joined by another nun, a Sister Margaret, not one of Sharon's, but the foundress of yet another new American order.

We gossiped on the piazza until Sister Margaret arrived, a short, plump woman in her forties with pink cheeks, bright eyes, and a cheerful smile. But what struck me most about her was her habit. She wore a full-length, traditional habit with wimple and veil, but in a surprisingly loud shade of royal blue. Sharon's Dior knockoff looked subtly chic beside it.

We had been strolling through the gardens for half an hour, when Kasia began studying Sister Margaret with her "doctor" look. I wondered what was up. "Sister Margaret, you are tired," she said.

"Me? No, no, I'm great."

"Does your leg hurt?"

"No, not at all. It never hurts now."

"You are tired," Kasia repeated firmly. "There is a place to sit up ahead. We will rest in the shade." She sounded like her mother. It was a tone that got results.

So we sat down on a low wall in the garden and the little nun in the blue habit told us this story.

Sister Margaret grew up in Philadelphia, a middle child in a large Catholic family. Her father was a police officer. Over the years he rose in the ranks to become a detective. He specialized in organized crime.

Her mother had a great devotion to Padre Pio, the stigmatist and healer of the Abbey of San Giovanni Rotundo, then still alive but already reputed a saint. During the long nights when her husband was working on often dangerous assignments, Margaret's mother would read to her children about Pio. Margaret grew to share her mother's devotion.

Before she moved to the Midwest to found her new convent, Margaret had been a teaching sister in a high school. One day, after classes, she and a group of students were decorating the gym for a dance. The students had devised an elaborate decorating scheme, part of which required hanging posters very high on the walls. They had an extension ladder but Margaret was both leery of letting any of her charges climb it and loathe to disappoint the kids, who had worked so hard. So Margaret decided she would be the one to go up the ladder. She was some fifteen feet above the ground when she slipped.

It seemed to take a very long time to fall to the floor. But Margaret did not get to review her whole life flashing before her eyes because all she could think of was how ridiculous she looked. "I mean, there I was, a nun in a full habit, falling off a ladder. Talk about an assault on my vanity," she recalled. "It's hard enough to win the respect of high school kids when you're standing up. So I tried to salvage what I could of the situation. As soon as I hit the floor I jumped right up. The kids were all horrified. 'Sister! Are you all right?' 'Oh, yes. Absolutely. I'm fine. Now about those streamers . . .'"

A week went by. Margaret went about her business, apparently unhurt, to the astonishment of all. Then one morning she woke up in agony, pain shooting through her body. She threw back the blankets and saw, to her horror, that her leg had turned completely black.

"It's from the fall," her superior said. "It has to be the fall."

As the nuns would learn, in the immediate after-math of the fall Margaret's body had gone into a kind of shock. But as the days passed, the shock wore off, and the injuries inflicted that day began to make themselves felt.

It was the beginning of two years of medical hell. Margaret had shattered several bones and profoundly damaged the circulatory system in her leg. Despite several operations, months in bed, and countless hours of physical therapy the leg refused to heal. She wore every kind of cast invented: wet casts, air casts, plaster casts. Struck repeatedly with infections, making it more difficult to fight off the circulatory damage, finally the leg threatened to turn gangrenous. The doctors began to urge amputation.

Throughout the ordeal, she had prayed to Padre Pio for help, to no avail. Now she asked him for the strength to face losing her leg.

"One night, I was sitting up late doing some spiritual reading in my room. One of the sisters saw my light on and knocked on the door. She told me someone had given her a relic of Padre Pio, and she thought I might like to have it. I already had a couple of his relics, but it was so nice of her to think of me, so I just said thank you and she left. I didn't do anything special with the relic; I just kissed it and rested it on my leg—I had a wet cast by then—while I said a prayer. Then I put it away, turned off my light, and went to sleep."

XXII

The next morning Margaret woke up as usual, except that without thinking she did something she hadn't done for two years: she threw back the covers and casually swung her legs over the side of the bed. Then she felt something very odd. She looked down. Her cast had slipped off. She could see her whole leg for the first time in two years. It was still criss-crossed with scars from all the operations, but otherwise appeared completely normal.

Her shriek of surprise brought a nursing sister rushing into her room. "Get back into bed," she ordered. She examined the leg carefully. She frowned in thought, then made a fist, and punched Margaret's leg as hard as she could.

Margaret yelped, more in surprise than pain. "What did you do that for?" she howled.

"Did that hurt?" the sister asked.

"Of course it hurt!"

"I mean, how did it hurt? Like a punch, or like something worse?"

"Well—like a punch."

"Nothing worse?"

"No."

The nursing sister prodded the leg with her fingers. "How does it feel now?"

"Fine."

Margaret saw her surgeons repeatedly in the following weeks. No one could explain how the leg had been healed. In the end two of her doctors—one a fallen-away Catholic, the other a Jewish atheist—agreed to submit their testimony to Rome: there was, as far as they had been able to determine, no natural explanation for the sudden and complete healing of Margaret's leg. In the end it was chalked up to Padre Pio, an apparent miracle, and formed part of the case for his canonization.

"So that's why I'm here," she said. "They want to see me walk around without a cane. I told them I'd run up and down all Seven Hills if they wanted me to." She smiled.

There are many different ways to receive such a story. With joyful, burning faith, with polite indifference, with bold skepticism. On that lovely, springlike day, the most beautiful I can remember in that beautiful place, with light breezes fluttering the foliage and golden Mediterranean sunlight streaming around us, I sat and listened in furious despair.

I believed Margaret. I believe in miracles. Because I believed, when John was sick I turned to Padre Pio for help. Now as we sat there on the wall in the cool garden, listening to a story of a miracle, all I could feel was rage. As sweet dear Sister Margaret told her story, smiling her sweet dear smile, all I wanted to do was shake her. I wanted to scream. "That's real nice for you, but where was Padre Pio when John was dying? Where is he now when the kids cry for their father, when they want to know why their wonderful, brave, smart, perfect daddy had to die, when my sister is a widow before she's forty? Who cares about your stupid miracle? Where's mine?"

Margaret told us her story, beaming with health and the knowledge that God loved her personally. I sat on the wall, choked back tears, and raged in my mind. Another failure. But this time it wasn't just some stupid novel that didn't get published, or any one of the other myriad personal humiliations I had begun to think made up the essence of my life. It was not even not having the baby, my first big failure in the miracle game. This time John died. Why? Because I wasn't on the miracle list?

As she finished her story—not without many interruptions from her little audience—Margaret announced, "I brought something to show you." She reached into her deep nun's habit pocket for a small cloth purse. Out of it she pulled a black woolen glove.

"This glove was worn by Padre Pio," she announced, explaining it had been given to her by an associate of Pio's who knew of Margaret's story.

We took turns examining the glove, really more of a "mitt," without fingertips. In photographs Pio can be seen wearing such a mitt, which he used so he could handle the objects used in the mass without exposing the wounds of Christ he bore on his hands. It was not made to be pulled on over the hand, but rather had a zipper up the side. Because of the wounds Pio's hands were often swollen and pulling a glove on the usual way would have been very painful.

At the wrist-end of the glove a chunk of wool was missing, a neat square evidently cut from the glove with a scissor. "What happened there?" I asked.

"Oh, that." Sister Margaret rolled her eyes. A few years back Margaret had shown the glove to another sister from a cloistered order. The nun oohed and ahhed and begged Margaret to let her borrow it just for a day or so, to show the other nuns in her convent. Margaret agreed but when the glove was returned the chunk was missing. With not a whiff of apology the other nuns smiled and cooed that they were sure Margaret would want their convent, so devoted to Padre Pio, to have just a teeny piece of such a wonderful relic. As the pilfering nuns surely knew, Sister Margaret was forbidden under her vows of poverty to own anything and in no position to complain. Margaret shrugged.

The most remarkable thing about the glove was the powerful scent of roses emanating from the wool.

The "odor of sanctity" has been the object of remarkably consistent testimony since at least the early Middle Ages. It may be the single most commonly witnessed of all miracles, with perhaps tens, or, who knows, hundreds of thousands experiencing it over the ages, though of course that still makes it fantastically rare. St. Paul uses fragrance as a metaphor for true knowledge of God and describes spreading this fragrance as the chief aim of his ministry. "But thanks be to God, who in Christ always leads us in triumph, and through us spreads the fragrance of the knowledge of him everywhere."

The wounds of St. Francis of Assisi were said to have emitted a pleasant scent sometimes, as were the exhumed bodies of saints like Teresa of Avila. Padre Pio himself made light of the phenomenon—"sweets for the children," he called it—but almost everyone who ever encountered Padre Pio had some experience of it, and no one ever forgot it.

When I used to hear about the odor of sanctity, I always wondered how I would recognize it for sure, since everyone always says it's like the scent of roses.

No problemo. It is like roses, but more powerful, and peculiarly heavy. Too heavy for me; I later confessed to Kasia with some embarrassment that I didn't really like the odor of sanctity. "Of course not," she replied matter-of-factly. "No one does." She told me that when Sister Margaret brought the glove to breakfast that morning, people kept surreptitiously moving it toward the open window. (The Holy Father was not at breakfast, Margaret told us, or she would not have brought the glove. The Church is very careful about miracles and Margaret sensed it would not be playing fair to wave one in the pontiff's face, unofficially as it were, and wait for his reaction.)

Margaret recounted the many times she had tested the authenticity of the scent: she had washed it by hand, laundered it in the washing machine, sent it to the dry cleaners. Still the scent remained, and it remained unchanged. Even if any perfume could be so persistent, and I have never encountered one, it almost certainly would have gone rancid.

It is said to be a grace to be able to smell the odor of sanctity. Not everyone does. Of course I had a brief anguished moment in which I thought, "Oh, God—what if everyone else smells it and not me? What would that say about me?" Luckily before I could even think about faking it, the smell just about knocked me over. Kasia told me the only one who couldn't smell it that morning at breakfast was her mother, *La Dottoressa*. The scientist.

What kind of God would think up such a thing? The God who formed from mud men of flesh and called them his "image and likeness"? The God who through the incarnation of his Son set these men of mud above the angels? The God who sweated blood once, whose dirty feet needed to be washed, who spat in the dirt and smeared the mud on a man's eyes?

Is it that the sense least relied upon by most humans is also somehow less easily deceived? Is that why God picked this for his favorite party piece? People see apparitions, or flying saucers "with their own two eyes," and then other people tell them they are "seeing things." But you don't often hear "you are smelling things."

Suppose you did what Sister Margaret said she did. Suppose you took this glove and learned its story and learned all about perfumes and wool and how it holds odors or doesn't. And you washed the glove, dry cleaned it, covered it in endless changes of baking soda, took it to a de-scenting specialist, and did everything possible to eliminate the scent of roses. And it still smelled exactly the same. And no scent expert in the world could explain it.

What then? What would you believe because of this miraculous smell? Would you believe in God? Would you believe He created the heavens and the Earth? Would you believe in His only Son, Jesus Christ? That He was conceived of the Holy Spirit, born of the Virgin Mary, suffered, died, and was buried, descended into hell and rose again on the third day? That He ascended into heaven where He sits at the right of the Father from whence He shall come again in glory to judge the living and the dead?

Or what?

Men speak. Dogs communicate by smell. Smell is an awkward, even impolite word. Children giggle at it. We say "aroma" when we intend a compliment but "what's that smell?" when we want to leave the room. Is the odor of sanctity, like so much of Christianity, a deliberate assault on primness, on vanity, on decorum? The Eucharist is incredibly awkward. Never mind that you stick out your tongue for it; there is also the minor point that according to Catholic doctrine you are eating the flesh and blood of the ever-living God, Creator of the Universe. And you think the Hare Krishnas are hard to take?

The Crucifixion wasn't just cruel and painful. It was ugly and undignified and humiliating. It was meant to be. Roman citizens could not be crucified because the indignity to Rome could not be tolerated. Provincials like Jesus were another story.

Christ couldn't carry his own cross. He fell three times. Romantic heroes don't do that. He was "stripped of his garments," and, no, that probably wasn't done in the discreet way it is usually portrayed. The Romans weren't in the business of sparing their victims or their families any humiliation. He sweat. And no doubt He stank.

XXIII

The last time we ever saw him in person was the following Sunday. Once again the streets were wet and slippery with the morning mist, but this year I had left my heels at home. My (perfectly presentable) sandals held their grip on the cobblestones wonderfully, not at all like that first morning when I feared I would break my neck, the morning that now seemed long ago. I had no "mission" this time, no Polaroid in my purse, no burning hopes in my heart. I felt quiet and calm and empty.

On the square a crowd of people stood outside the palace gate, waiting their turn to go in for Sunday mass on the palace courtyard. A security man waved to Richard, and we slipped in beside him.

The courtyard was transformed for the mass. Hundreds of chairs were lined up in neat rows, and blocks of what were obviously pilgrimage groups filled most of them.

There was a big group of Girl Guides from France. Dark blue berets, bright bandanas, and an outdoorsy look. They sat in the front section, holding little leaflets in their hands.

There were other groups too: university fellowships, professional associations. Some Germans or Swiss wearing lederhosen and singing oom-pah-pah music. Most stunning was a group of fifty or sixty Vietnamese pilgrims sitting ramrod straight in their chairs, silent, waiting for mass to begin. The men wore business suits; the women wore traditional high-collared, close-fitting silk gowns over matching trousers. Pink, peach, sapphire, turquoise. Like a jungle garden.

The mass began. Holy Father joined as usual by a crowd of priest concelebrants. I recognized a few: the secretary, Holy Father's cheerful friend Father Tadeusz, the little Vietnamese monsignor who had led us through the palace labyrinth the morning of the Confirmation. A reunion.

The French Girl Guides sang the responsorial psalm and a couple of hymns as well, all *a cappella*. The girls sang very prettily and right on key.

Once again the pope refrained from passing out Holy Communion; once again, when Communion was finished, he sat down and propped his chin on his fist, a faint smile playing at his lips, lost in contemplation. The Holy Father stood up; the final blessing was given. The mass was over.

"There you are." Kasia materialized by my side. "I'm sorry I missed you. We were at the back. The boys just could not get out of bed this morning. They stayed up too late last night."

"Doing what?"

"Singing, mostly. Holy Father stopped by the apartment."

"Sounds like fun."

"It is. We've been doing it for years, you know, before he was elected. If only we could have had a campfire it would have been perfect. Oh, and I have to tell you. When we were all done he left, then just a minute later he was back. He just leaned inside the door to reach for . . . a last brownie from the mantlepiece. He held it up and smiled and said, 'New York?'"

In our house, those have been "Papal Brownies" ever since.

Kasia glanced back over her shoulder and waved to someone. "That's my mother. I've got to run inside. Stan and the boys will take you up, after the morning audience."

A burst of applause announced the pontiff's return to the courtyard. The men of the Zajac family folded their arms and stood back to watch the pope's progress.

There were several groups of students; one was from some college in Poland. As the pope approached them the group burst into song. A broad smile spread across John Paul's face, and he sang along with them for a minute. The students loved it.

When the pope came to the Girl Guides the first

thing he did was seek out the girl who'd led the singing and give her a kiss on the forehead. She laughed, looking incredibly happy. She brightened even more when the pope said something to her; he must have asked for another song because she immediately gave the others a signal and pulled out her pitchpipe. They sang. The pope applauded them; they applauded him.

At last the Holy Father came to the Vietnamese. I realized that I had been waiting for this. The women were so beautiful, the men so intent. The word "passion" kept coming to mind, as in passion play, which of course made no sense at all.

Holy Father spoke to the group as a whole and then to some privately. When he finally moved on a lady in a pearl white gown suddenly lunged forward, running after the pope as if her life depended on it. Her hands were outstretched before her, in a pitiful gesture of supplication.

She was holding a photograph. She was trying to show it to the pope.

Before she could get close the Vietnamese monsignor intercepted her. She showed him the picture; he nodded; he spoke to her soothingly. But he did not let her get near the pontiff again.

Now many of the Vietnamese were looking at the ground, as if shamed. I wondered if they had been worried that just this would happen. Had there been earnest discussions of the lady and her picture? Had they all been afraid she would embarrass them?

It wasn't embarrassing. It was love. It was desperate. And now what would the woman think over and over and over, when she got home to the other side of the world, when the husband or child, son or daughter in the picture died? Would she think, "I failed"? Would she think, "It's all my fault"?

I hoped not. I hoped she realized God already knew all about whomever it was in the picture.

The question was, Did he care?

"Here comes Holy Father," Stan said. "Charlie, behave."

"I always behave," he protested.

"Ah, New York!" The pope approached Richard with his hands outstretched. "Good to see you again!"

Richard beamed. He kissed the pope's ring with a minimum of ceremony and introduced me again. The pope shook my hand. I kissed his ring. Then John Paul turned to the boys. Walter and Charlie kissed the Holy Father's ring, just as their father did. Charlie's face, normally so full of passion and mischief, was all serenity as the pope touched his hair fondly and murmured something in Polish. The boys always seemed transformed in his presence, but not only the boys.

I had noticed it in photographs before, especially the ones of Richard and me, that no matter how awkward or self-conscious you thought you were feeling when you met him, in the photos you were always smiling in a way you were pretty sure you didn't usually. The picture of us meeting him that morning hangs in our kitchen. I went up to the palace that day with a deeply disappointed heart, but in the picture my smile is real. "I never saw you look happier," a friend said a few years later. I looked at the picture again myself and realized I had to agree.

The pope moved on pretty quickly; he would be seeing us upstairs, and there were more people waiting to meet him. We followed Stan into the palace.

Kasia and one of the nuns were fussing over the table setting when we arrived. "Italian breakfast this morning," Kasia whispered in my ear as she plunked some flowers into a vase. "So you can eat anything you want. Big change from last time!"

"Don't remind me," I groaned.

"OK, but just in case, the bathroom's right over —"

Once again Kasia's mother assigned seats, seizing us by the elbows and steering us over to our chairs. She sat Stan and Kasia across from us, toward the foot of the table. Kasia whispered, "Good, we can talk."

We all stood behind our chairs and waited. Then the pope arrived. Everyone clapped. He lifted his hands and smiled. "Buon giorno," he boomed, "e buon appetito!" The boys laughed. They loved this man.

After grace, which we said standing, a nun went around the table pouring coffee. Once again Kasia warned me away from it. But I had to try it once. "Oh, my God, yech."

"Told you."

Another nun came in with the pope's drink. Whatever it was it came in a huge white ceramic cup, the kind you'd expect to see "World's Greatest Grandpa" printed on the side. He nodded his thanks; the nun disappeared.

Breakfast was subdued. At first I thought it was because Sharon wasn't there; subdued didn't happen much around her. But soon I had the feeling something else was up. Holy Father was as friendly and generous a host as always, but he seemed distracted.

Suddenly the pope looked to the boys and asked, "Do you know what day it is today?"

"It's the first of August," Charlie piped up.

The Holy Father nodded gravely. "August first." Then to Richard and me, including us. "It is a grave day for us, an anniversary."

A heavy, haunted look fell on the Poles. Their heads drooped, their eyes seemed to lose their focus. The first of August, 1944, the Warsaw uprising. For months the Germans had been in retreat before the advancing Russian army, which now sat just across miles from Poland's capital on the eastern side of the Vistula. There were twenty maybe thirty thousand German soldiers occupying the city, including tanks, artillery, and air support. But why would the Germans, who had been retreating for months, make a stand in Warsaw? Convinced they could end the war now, at least for Poland, the Polish Home Army, a few thousand ill-equipped militia, rose up against the Germans sure that the Russians on the far bank would move to their support and the Germans woud swiftly decamp.

Instead Hitler gave the order to hold Warsaw at all costs. The Russians sat on their hands and watched the slaughter.

The fighting lasted sixty-three days. German soldiers entered the city's hospitals and murdered patients in their beds, burning the bodies to destroy the evidence; wounded Polish insurgents were burned alive in field hospitals. Women were used as human shields in front of advancing Nazi tanks. The Russians refused to allow the Allies to use their airfields even to drop supplies to the Poles. Estimates of civilian Polish dead ranged from one hundred twenty thousand to over two hundred thousand. The Polish Home Army was annihilated. The Germans burned much of what was left of the city even after the fighting, exiling the entire population, many to forced labor camps. When the Red Army finally entered Warsaw, in January 1945, the city was a ruin.

No one had been thinking about defeat on August 1, 1944. Everywhere was wild hope.

"We thought the war was over," Kasia's father said. "We heard all about it in Cracow, and we hoped—we hoped!"

La Dottoressa nodded. "Even in the camps we heard.

Warsaw was all anyone could talk about. We were so sure."

Holy Father looked at Richard. "I was in Cracow." He extended a finger and gestured toward his old friend. "And she was in Ravensbrück."

Poor, dumb, shy Americans. What can we do or say at this horrible moment? Anything to keep from crossing over into the real world, the world of the spirit, of human frailties and triumphs, and of all the horrible messy imperious emotions demanding our honor. Like children who do not yet know what suffering is, in sheer panic we change the subject.

"It's our wedding anniversary today!" we respond. The others around the table quickly smile and offer polite congratulations. The moment is lost. Reality slips away. The Holy Father, back on duty, motions to an attendant, who slips out of the room and reappears moments later with little gifts for Richard and me.

It's hard to write this part; I feel so foolish. If only I'd kept my mouth shut, what more might I have learned from those survivors of history? Instead, terrified I made them stop sharing the brutal truth with me. How many times I've wished I could live that moment over again and get it right this time.

Why do I waste so much time? What's the point of life if not to face the truth? This deep, peculiarly American shyness, this jollying our way out of facing the hard parts, is not charming or gay or carefree. It's a tragedy.

It kills the soul, or at least stops it in its tracks. Just as the journey might begin, it cracks a joke, flicks on the TV, raises the most sensible and practical objections. Perhaps it would be better to go another time after all.

I come back here to Italy again and again in part for the deep reality, to surround myself with passionate wholeness in this place where body and soul are still united, to let go of the fear of life that can waste a life. And I know that Italy would do this for me, if I gave it a chance and had a little courage.

It's funny, but my favorite line from Scripture is also the line John Paul has made the theme of his papacy: "Be not afraid." Christ says it over and over again in different ways. It's the heart of his teaching. It would have to be for any religion in which the Crucifixion is a moment of triumph and the day of execution is called "Good." Christ spent his entire life grabbing people by the lapels and telling them, "Live as you were meant to, fully and with abandon. What have you got to lose except your regrets?"

That's the kind of life I want.

The rosaries Holy Father gave us for an anniversary gift are beautiful. I keep them not in my regular jewelry box left out conveniently for burglars with limited imagination but in the hidey hole where I stash a few things I really don't want them to get. The beads were finished in pearl. The crucifix is the distinctive one carved for John Paul's papacy, Christ's body showing every effect of days of torture, twisted in pain, muscles spasming, emaciated like a concentration-camp victim, head fallen on his chest, nothing left but endurance.

"Be not afraid."

Richard thanked the Holy Father for both of us.

ℬ • ℛ

Unfortunately it is not possible to throw money into an Italian fountain without thinking of that awful cloying song. But I never let that stop me from making a wish on my last night in Italy.

I stood in front of Bernini's little marble fountain, jingling the change in my hand, trying to think of something to wish for.

I wish I knew why.

My handful of lire splashed in the fountain. A couple of kids stuck their hands into the water and scooped up the change, then ran off, laughing.

We made it to the airport in plenty of time, but we were still bumped from our flight.

Actually we volunteered to be bumped. In exchange for a few hours' wait for another plane we scored two vouchers for free flights anywhere in the world. "This way we know we'll be back," Richard said. "Is that what you wished for in the fountain last night?"

"Not exactly," I said. "But it's good enough, for now."

XXIV

Whe we got home I wrote it all down. At first it was just therapy: me trying to make sense of John and God and my faith and my life. Then it became something more, though I still did not speak of it, not even to Richard. Finally, in November I think, I told Richard rather shyly, "I think I have a book."

Richard read it and told me that finally this was the writer he'd married, the writer he'd always known was there, but had been hiding behind my too artfully chosen words for years. This time there was no hiding. I called Sharon and told her about it, a little hesitantly because I was afraid she might think a story about not getting one's miracle might be, as the nuns say, "unedifying." Instead I got just the opposite reaction. "People need to hear what faith is really like in real life," she told me, then asked if I had a title. I told her *Breakfast with the Pope*, and she nearly shrieked, "It will sell!"

But Kasia I had to tell in person. It was more than half the reason we had come back to Italy.

Castel Gandolfo gets very quiet in the afternoons,

and it is easy to sleep through siesta. By the time Richard and I were awake and showered and dressed again it was nearly five o'clock. Too early for dinner and too late for much else. Luckily, it is always the right time for lounging on the piazza. So that's where we went.

No sooner had we established ourselves at a table than Richard spotted them. Kasia, Stan, and the two boys emerged from one of the square's cafés. Behind them were Kasia's parents and an older man in clerical dress, the visiting bishop, I guessed.

Richard stood up and waved. "Walter! Charlie!"

The boys looked up. When they saw us, they both looked startled. They looked at each other, then at Kasia, but Kasia was busy talking to the bishop. The boys looked confused. They did not wave back.

Richard got up and went over to them. "Hey, guys! Good to see you!"

"Oh, um—hello, Uncle Richard." Charlie was distant, polite. "I didn't know you'd be here this year."

"Well, of course, we are!" Now Richard looked confused. This was hardly the greeting he'd been looking forward to.

Behind them Kasia was hanging back. Smiling, but distant, as if we were meeting for the first time. "Hi," I said. "How are you?"

"I am well, thank you." She sounded stiff.

"Can you have dinner?" I asked.

"Oh, no. We must get back."

"Uh, OK, well . . . what about later? Can we see you after dinner?"

"I'm afraid not. We have a guest, as you can see."

Suddenly Stan intervened. "No, not tonight. The bishop is leaving in an hour, remember?"

Kasia shot him a look. Stan fell silent.

"Well, if you're busy, I know . . . ," I was foundering. "Can I call you tomorrow?"

"I'm afraid we won't have much free time this week. Now we must go. Walter, Charlie. Come."

No one could have missed the imperative in Kasia's tone. The boys followed their mother up the cobblestone ramp and through the gate. Stan hesitated briefly before saying good-bye and following his wife.

"Maybe they had a fight," Richard theorized over dinner. "Or maybe Kasia was fighting with her mother. Or Stan was. It could have been anything."

I said nothing.

Richard sighed. "Look, let's just go back to the piazza after dinner. Maybe they'll come out and they'll be in a better mood."

We had been there about two hours when who should come strolling across the piazza but Sister Stephen Marie and her colleague, Sister John Paul.

I should have known right then that something was wrong. I should have known, because for the first time since I met her, I felt no joy at seeing Sharon. I didn't know what I felt. Later I decided it was suspicion.

"When did you get here?" I demanded, when the two nuns had sat down at our table.

"About a week ago," said Sharon.

"A little longer, actually," Sister John Paul said, then looked chagrined.

"Why didn't you tell me you were coming?"

"Oh, we wanted to surprise you," Sharon said vaguely.

Before I could ask any more questions she and Sister John Paul started talking about how they'd been driving in Rome earlier, how tiny their rental car was, joking about what a terrible driver Sharon still was. They were "making conversation." Never in my life had I "made conversation" with Sharon. I listened with half an ear. Most of my attention was focused on the palace gate.

Not fifteen minutes after Sharon arrived the heavy oak doors creaked open, and Kasia and her husband stepped out. I watched as she and Sharon made unsmiling eye contact. I thought I saw Kasia nod.

Sharon turned to me quickly. "Have you talked to Kasia about your book yet?"

"No," I said. "I haven't been able to get hold of her. I didn't see her until tonight . . ."

"But you're going to tell her now, aren't you?"

"No," I said quickly. "Not now."

At this Sharon looked disapprovingly, but as Kasia was just about to sit down she said nothing.

"Well." Richard sat back and looked around the table. "Here we are again! My favorite people in my favorite place."

The nuns smiled stiffly. Kasia scanned a menu.

"So what have you been doing?" he asked.

"Oh, the usual," Sister John Paul replied. "Paperwork, you know. You wouldn't believe how much of it there is."

"We did get to mass in St. Peter's today," said Sharon. "That was nice."

"Are you staying at the Castelvecchio?"

"Yes."

I could see Richard was running out of conversation starters, so I tried a few. "Have you been up to the palace yet?" I asked. "Have you seen Holy Father?"

There was a brief silence as Kasia, Sharon, and Sister John Paul exchanged glances. Finally Sharon said, "Oh, you know, it's been hit or miss."

I turned to Kasia. "Did your bishop leave?"

She nodded. "Yes, . . . but Holy Father has so many guests. We are busy this year."

The conversation crawled along like that for perhaps half an hour. Then Sister John Paul reminded Sharon they had to finish some correspondence before they turned in. Sharon waved good-bye over her shoulder as the two of them walked back across the piazza toward their hotel.

Finally Kasia stood up. "We must go also," she

announced. Stan looked like he was about to protest, but one look from his wife silenced him. He stood up. Then he turned to Richard and shook his hand. "Good night," he said. "Enjoy your stay."

When we got back to the Bucci there was a note taped to our door:

Sue. Be at the Castelvecchio at ten. We have to talk. Sharon.

In the morning Richard and I called at the Hotel Castelvecchio. The desk clerk told us the American nun was waiting on the patio where breakfast was served.

The patio overlooked the lake. This time of day it was in full sun. Sharon waved to us from a table.

"This is the only shade I could find," she said. "Have a seat. I've ordered some coffee."

"Thank you." I sat down. I had the odd feeling I had been summoned to Sharon's office.

She got right down to business. "We have to talk about your book."

"Oh?"

"You can't publish it, Sue."

My mouth fell open. "What?"

"I said, you can't publish this book. Not without Kasia's full cooperation and permission, and I should warn you she isn't inclined to give it."

"You told her about the book?"

Sharon looked around vaguely. "I wasn't the first," she said. "She'd already heard."

"From whom?"

"I'd rather not say." She pointed a finger at me. "You're going to tell Kasia about the book today, and you're going to ask her permission to go forward with it and if she says no you are going to drop it."

I stared at her, shocked. I must have said something, probably pretty nasty, but I can't remember what. I got to my feet. Richard said quietly, "I think you should stay, Sue."

All I could get out was, "I want to be alone."

I fled.

The confrontation had been brief, loud, and public. More than anything I hate being a spectacle. I didn't want to be seen up at the piazza or at the Bucci with this stricken look on my face. The church would be closed now, and I was too shaken to drive down to the lake on my own. So I found the shop that sold silk scarves and went down into the cool, stone cellar where the pottery was. I stayed there for nearly an hour.

When I had calmed down I went back to our room. Richard was there, stretched out on the bed, waiting for me.

"Sharon sent you this." He held out a tiny folded square of paper. I read the note and put it away in my purse.

"What's it say?"

"Tell you later." Suddenly I felt exhausted, but the prospect of lying around the Bucci gave me a sick, stale feeling. "Could we go down to the lake?"

"I'm ready."

At the beach he said, "We don't have to talk about it yet, if you don't want to. But whenever you feel up to it I'm here."

"Thank you." I could barely speak.

I lay down on my back. The heat of the black volcanic sand seeped through my towel and spread through my neck and shoulders, warming my stiff muscles and soothing my frayed nerves, a little—enough, at least, to let me think about the events of the morning.

How could Sharon turn on me like that? What happened to "it will sell!"? All the encouragement she'd given me over the years—was it all a lie? How could anyone object to a book they hadn't read a page of?

And what did they think I wrote the book for? All the hours I'd spent with them here—did they think I was just gathering material? I loved them. I thought they loved me. Did they even know me?

I fumbled in my purse for her note and reread it in the bright sunlight.

"What's it say?" Richard asked.

"It says she regrets upsetting me," I said. "And that she is sure I will do the right thing in the end."

I looked at Richard. "I never felt more lost in my life," I said.

As soon as we got back I went straight to the palace. The porter came out to the gate; I asked him if I could use the telephone. He ushered me into the small office: a desk, a chair, a phone, a crucifix on the wall, something vaguely familiar playing on the radio. I listened for a moment. It was Madonna singing "Beautiful Stranger."

The porter smiled and gestured at the radio. "Bella voce, eh?"

"Si. Molto bella."

He ushered me to the chair like a maître d' showing me to his best table, handed me the receiver, and stepped outside to smoke a cigarette.

Kasia answered on the third ring. I tried not to believe she had been sitting by the phone per Sharon's instructions, waiting for a call.

"Kasia? We have to talk."

"Yes."

"Can you meet me tonight on the piazza? After dinner?"

"Yes."

"OK. I'll see you later."

She hung up. Not even "good-bye."

I put the phone back. I had a sick feeling in my stomach.

As I left the palace I heard footsteps behind me. "Signora! Signora!"

I stopped. It was the porter. He looked worried. "Signora—tutti OK?"

"Oh, yes—si."

He looked at me closely. "Certo?"

"Si. I'm sure. Thank you."

It was late. The piazza was crowded with café tables; the steps of San Tommaso were strewn with pairs of lounging young lovers, and a gaggle of high school kids stood around the Bernini fountain, trying to appear blasé.

"There they are," Richard said.

Kasia gave me a peck on the cheek before she sat down, all bright smiles and polite inquiries: Had we been to the lago? Was the Bucci crowded? Were we planning any side trips? Stan looked tired and depressed. The boys were not with them.

We had a carafe of wine, but no one was drinking. I asked Kasia if she would come for a walk with me. The men looked a little surprised at this—what are we supposed to do now?—but Kasia said "yes," a walk was a good idea. So we went off together.

We were barely off the square when I said, "Kasia, it's very important that you listen to me."

She nodded and folded her arms.

"OK. I know you've heard that I've been working on a book . . ."

"It must never be published."

"Kasia. Please, listen. I don't know what you could have heard about it, but you really have nothing to worry about . . ."

"How dare you!" Kasia's eyes were full of wrathful indignation. "How dare you take advantage of our friendship! It is a great privilege to meet the Holy Father and if it weren't for me you never would have had it! How dare you throw it back in my face like this!"

"Kasia, I'm not . . ."

"The *treachery*, Susan! The treachery of it! Going off behind my back like this! You are a traitor! You have betrayed my friendship!"

"Please, don't say that . . ."

"You never said a word to me! Everyone else knew all about this book before I did!"

"Kasia, nobody knows anything about it! I haven't shown any of it to anyone!"

"Well I know what it's about! I don't care what you say! This book must never be published, Susan. Never. Do you understand?"

A traitor. A betrayer. A false friend. I wasn't. I wasn't. I wasn't. But she believed it. I am so terrible at this sort of thing. Richard might have been able to talk her down, spread oil on the waters. But I was helpless and tongue-tied and sure I would make it worse if I opened my mouth. The full despair of the moment hit me hard, and in the middle of the street I burst into tears. "Fine," I shouted. "Fine. You know so much about it, why don't you write your own book?"

And I ran. All the way back to the Bucci. Sobbing.

The next day Richard did try. He talked to Stan

and told him that we were sorry about the misunderstanding and that we would be happy for him and Kasia to read the manuscript and remove anything they thought was improper or might hurt their relationship with the Holy Father. Stan said they did not want to be our censors. Richard thought that such an odd response that he went to Sharon and repeated the same offer, sure that she would see this as a peaceful resolution.

Sharon refused in a way that shocked and angered him. Later he told me that he could not remember Sharon's exact words, but, he explained, "what she said to me basically was that this offer to let them read the book was a trick. She told me essentially 'the only reason you want to do that is you think that if they read the book they will like it and give in.' I had no idea what to say to that because I do think that. I think if they would just read it they'd love it and we'd all be laughing about it on the piazza. How is that a trick? I think they would like it because it's beautiful. How is it a trick to show someone something good?"

Richard's brother Kevin, also traveling in Italy that summer, arrived the next morning. We told him what had happened, and he understood when we said we didn't feel we could stay in Castel Gandolfo much longer. The next day the three of us would leave for Siena, where Kevin was joining an archeological dig.

The last time I saw Sharon was on the piazza. I was coming out of the post office, where I had changed some money for the drive to Tuscany, heading over to the fountain for a last look. She and Sister John Paul were walking toward the palace. Sister John Paul gave me a big wave; Sharon gave me a practiced smile. But they didn't stop. And we didn't speak.

I was to meet Richard and Kevin at the Bucci in ten minutes for the drive to Siena. But as I turned away from the sisters, my heart breaking, my eyes fell on San Tommaso and I was drawn inside.

I knelt to pray, head down, but I couldn't. Instead I stared at the great altar setting, one of the most dramatic of all Bernini's creations.

Above the altar is a very large oval painting of the Crucifixion by the artist Pietro da Cortona. Vivid and powerful, Jesus is just at the point of death mourned by his mother, the Magdalene, and St. John.

They are not the only mourners. Bernini had taken the painting as an inspiration and surrounded it by mourners in stone. And since this is Bernini they are mourners in living stone. The frame of the painting is held up by two angels, one on the right and one on the left at the bottom of the oval. Clinging to one of the angels is a naked cherub. Although the angels clearly have to be there as witnesses to the Crucifixion, their faces are turned away, their eyes cast downward as if they cannot bear to look.

On the right side of the oval near the top a little marble cherub clings to the frame, one chubby arm reaching onto the portrait itself. The cherub's head is on the same level as that of the crucified Jesus, and the baby face looks at Christ with an expression of mystified sorrow, like a child seeing something it doesn't understand but knows is wrong.

Christ suffers. Mary suffers. John and the angels are in anguish. But they are not alone.

For above the painting is a marble figure of God the Father. It is in some ways a traditional portrayal, with long beard and flowing robes. But there is no serenity here. No stately, majestic hovering in the heavens. He has left heaven behind, hurtling through space—down, down, down, his robe streaming back behind him, his arms outstretched—toward Golgotha. He has seen the suffering of His Son and He has charged down from heaven. He reaches out to Jesus. The outstretched hands are full of horrified vitality, the fingers spread, the tendons taut with anguish. This is a Father watching His own child, His little boy, being tortured.

And not watching only. For it is near the end now and He has heard, heard His child scream out in pain the most devastating words that any parent can imagine in his worst nightmare. *Daddy, where are you!* "Eli, Eli, lama sabachthani!" Why have you abandoned me!

He hates it. He hates every inch of it, every breath of it, every second of it. But still He does not intervene. In the end, at the last possible moment, hurtling through the air, He stops. He does not allow Himself to enter the scene, to storm into Jerusalem and reveal His power. He watches in unfathomable grief as His Son fulfills His destiny. He pays a price just as His Son did, and who is to say the Father's wasn't greater?

He didn't want it either. He didn't want His Son to die.

He never planned it this way. He made us to be with Him, body and soul. *Body* and soul. Death was never in the blueprints. That was somebody else's bright idea.

You hated it, too, I thought. You hate it as much as we do.

And then I wept and wept.

Epilogue I

Over time I made two decisions. The book was good. Not just a good book but a good thing. I would finish it and publish it.

I could not give in, even for Sharon.

No. That's not right. I could not give in *because* of Sharon. To let myself be bullied out of doing this good thing would end our friendship just as surely as standing my ground, but end it in a lie. The Sharon I knew and loved could never tolerate a lie.

I could, however, wait. If Kasia felt so strongly that the book might in some way endanger her relationship with the Holy Father, or—as I thought more likely—bring down on her the wrath of her mother, then I could wait for years, even. I would not do it as a concession to her, but I could do it for her.

The other decision I made was not to disbelieve. I don't mean in God. For whatever bizarre reason, I am never seriously tempted by atheism. I mean in Sharon, and my love for her, and her love for me. I knew that I had loved her. I knew that love is real. And nothing will ever persuade me that she had not loved me.

Sharon was real. Her love was real. But we are not God. Our love is not perfect. For us sometimes love means choosing. When that moment came, Sharon did not choose me.

Her choice did not make our past a lie. To say, because she did not choose me in the end, that I had never had her love, would have been a terrible betrayal of all she had been to me, all she had taught me and given me, all that I had become with her.

Thinking of Sharon I had asked, all those years ago, "Is that what mothers do?"

And she had done it. I had in so many ways grown up under her protection.

I was grown up.

And so, she was free to choose. And she did choose. And I could walk away knowing she would never be there for me again, but that would be OK.

If that's not real, I don't know what is.

Epilogue II

On August 19, 2001, by the order of the King and the People of Cambodia, in the province of Phnom Penh, and one day ahead of schedule because we could not wait another minute, the orphan girl Sorphea Rath, 362 days old, became Sophia Teresa Vigilante.

Epilogue III

On the second of April 2005, John Paul the Great died. It was the Saturday of Easter week. He was eighty-four years old; he had been pope for twenty-six years.

The Requiem Mass was said on St. Peter's Square. When the mass drew to a close, a handful of men in black picked up John Paul's simple wooden coffin and marched slowly up the steps of the great Basilica. At the top of the stairs they stopped. Slowly, slowly, they turned around and showed the crowd the coffin one last time. John Paul II was saying good-bye. Alone in front of the television, I burst into tears.

Good-bye, Holy Father. Good-bye. Thank you for everything. Thank you for your smile and your wonderful wit, for your great heart and your lousy coffee. Thank you from the bottom of my heart. You have many friends in heaven. One of them is named John—you remember. You'll like him. Tell him I said hello.